Continuity and Change:
INDIA'S FOREIGN POLICY

Continuity and Change: INDIA'S FOREIGN POLICY

IK GUJRAL

MACMILLAN

First published, 2003

MACMILLAN INDIA LTD.
Delhi Chennai Jaipur Mumbai Patna
Bangalore Bhopal Chandigarh Coimbatore Cuttack
Guwahati Hubli Hyderabad Lucknow Madurai
Nagpur Pune Raipur Siliguri Thiruvananthapuram Visakhapatnam

Companies and representatives throughout the world

ISBN 0333 93681 7

Published by Rajiv Beri for Macmillan India Ltd.
2/10 Ansari Road, Daryaganj, New Delhi 110002

Lasertypeset by V.S. Calligraphics Pvt. Ltd.
16/863 Joshi Road, Karol Bagh, New Delhi 110005

Printed at Replika Press, India.

India's Foreign Policy as Some World Leaders Saw It

You, as a mature and experienced statesman and formidable intellect who has been in the mainstream of Indian politics over a major part of life guiding the destinies of your nation, have made unequivocal commitment to promote greater understanding, tolerance and friendship amongst the people of the world. Your effort bodes well for the future of the humanity.

You are admired as a leader of great wisdom and foresight and close friend of the people of Sri Lanka. Your continued counsel and support, therefore, would be invaluable in our effort towards nation building.

Chandrika Bandaranaike Kumaratunga
President, Sri Lanka

We are encouraged by your deep and continuing commitment to the process of opening a dialogue with Pakistan on the issues that are problematic in your relations, including over Kashmir. I am encouraged in particular by the courage and foresight you have shown in your effort to achieve a settlement with Pakistan and to open a new and brighter chapter in the history of the region. You have our full support and backing in this endeavor. We will of course respect the wishes of the parties in regard to what role we can play in this process.

William J. Clinton
President, USA

I still have in mind the very warm welcome that you extended to me during my State visit to India, last January, for the Republic Day celebrations of the 50th anniversary of your Independence. I was very touched by the personal gestures of friendship that you had lavished on me and by the quality and the density of our dialogue. I am pleased that together we were able to take Indo-French partnership to a very high level and to decide to strengthen it in all fields. Your personal commitment towards Indo-French relations has enabled spectacular developments in our relation. We will have to work more towards it continuously so that France and India truely become two great special partners.

The high level political dialogue between France and India seems to me essential on all major international political issues. That is why I wished to dispatch to you Ambassador Denis Bauchard to present to you the French position in the presidential palaces' crisis in Iraq and to obtain your analyses. I was very touched by the fact that you personally received him. He gave me an account of your analyses and your messages and I incorporated them in the framework of my own reflections regarding the continuation of our action.

I wish to finally pay a special tribute to your courage as well as to the very wise and sensible policy that you followed in the execution of your high duties.

Jacques Chirac
President, France

Over the last years the Russian-Indian relations have made significant progress. There is undoubtedly your personal contribution to it as the head of the Government of India and Minister of External Affairs. We are proud to regard you as a true friend of our country.

Over these years India has gained ever greater respect of the international community. The foreign policy doctrine, which appropriately bears your name, has already brought about tangible results and strengthened the hope and faith of millions of men and women in South Asia in better future. A trend towards building an atmosphere of good neighborly relations and mutual understanding has clearly emerged in the vast Indian sub-continent.

E. Primakov
Prime Minister, Russia

You rendered distinguished service to your country and, as your experience of Edinburgh would have demonstrated, your former colleagues value the role India continues to play in the Commonwealth and your own special contributions in this process. Your period in office provided me with some of my most valuable moments of collaboration with your country and I much valued your kindness, wise guidance and support.

Emeka Anyaoku
Secretary-General, The Commonwealth

I want to express my personal thanks for your insight, generosity of spirit, and goodwill as our nations have addressed the many challenges confronting them ... you did not shrink from the turbulent sea of foreign affairs but immersed yourself in an innovative foreign policy. I believe you will be long remembered for this spirit and for that policy. The 'Gujral Doctrine' is the most prominent feature, along with the resumption of dialogue between India and Pakistan and the creation of a new spirit of cooperation in the region. From my perspective I particularly commend the strides we made in relations between India and the United States.

Madeleine K. Albright
Secretary of State, USA

The British Government salute your contributions to the democratic process in the world's largest democracy. And we admire the real achievements of the Gujral Doctrine in fostering stability and growth in South Asia.

Tony Blair
Prime Minister, United Kingdom

I have great pleasure in recollecting my interaction with you as colleagues in the period that you have so successfully led India as your country's Prime Minister. I have been deeply touched by the affection that you have shown to me each time we met. In the process, I have grown to admire you for your many human qualities and your statesmanship in leading your own country as well as in dealing with India's neighbours.

As Prime Minister of India, you have done a great deal for the improvement of our bilateral relations. Indeed, your genuine spirit of cooperation made my task easier as I worked with you for the strengthening of our bilateral relations. The historic Ganges Water Sharing Treaty that we reached with India in December 1996, was possible to a large measure for the understanding that you personally demonstrated at a time when you were the External Affairs Minister of India. The same spirit was visible from you as Prime Minister as we dealt with the entire gamut of our bilateral relations. We have together brought our relations to a point where these show all the signs of developing both in content and character. As a result, our people consider you as a genuine friend of Bangladesh which was evident when you visited us in Dhaka in January 1998 during the Bangladesh, India, Pakistan Business Summit. In this context, I wish to acknowledge my personal indebtedness to you for making the Summit a successful one by your personal commitment.

Sheikh Hasina
Prime Minister, Bangladesh

Foreword

In his capacity as the Foreign Minister and then as the Prime Minister of India, it was the privilege of Shri I K Gujral to shape and conduct the foreign policy of India at a critical period when the world was undergoing rapid transition and India itself was in the throes of change. As the author says in the introduction to this book 'Jawaharlal Nehru's vision has bequeathed to India the broad paradigm of our foreign policy. Our task was to correlate it to the emerging scenarios.' Such correlation with the emerging and bewildering international and domestic scenarios was no ordinary task. Fortunately for India, the changes in the world— the collapse of the military blocs and the end of the cold war— did not render the basic approach of Non-Alignment outmoded and irrelevant. Nehru had said a few months before his passing away:

The basis of non-alignment is our area of peace which has been constantly expanding since the inception of the policy. As more and more nations keep joining this peace club as against the nuclear club and the cold war club, we expect the non-aligned group to grow and absorb other nations like France and Czechoslovakia which today belong to NATO and WARSAW pact military alliances. We want the whole world to become part of this area of peaceful co-operation including ultimately the United States and the Soviet Union.

Though the world did not change quite exactly as Nehru

ix

thought, the developments have been more along the lines of peaceful coexistence and cooperation advocated by the Non-Aligned rather than by the Aligned. Yet the complexities and the contradictions in the world situation as it emerged were such that it was not easy to apply the Nehruvian paradigm to contemporary scenarios. It called for a foreign policy of continuity and change combined. It is to the credit of Shri Gujral that he evolved a new framework of policy that was marked by creativity in its continuity.

This new framework of policy came to be known as the 'Gujral Doctrine'. The core of the new framework remained independence of thought and action in foreign affairs. The innovative part of it was the emphasis on relations with neighbours like Bangladesh, Bhutan, Maldives and Sri Lanka to whom we give what we can in good faith without asking for reciprocity. This idea of not insisting upon reciprocity helped in producing a new sense of trust in them at a time when India's relations with its neighbours had come under great stress. The examples of this policy were the trade arrangement with Nepal conceding transit to Bangladesh, and the River Water Treaty with Bangladesh. The Gujral Doctrine encouraged the SAARC initiative to establish a South Asian Free Trade Arrangement (SAFTA) by the year 2005 and to launch the South Asian Preferential Trade Agreement (SAPTA).

The Gujral Doctrine was not confined to the subcontinent but covered cooperation with India's extended neighbourhood—South East Asia, the Asia Pacific and the Indian Ocean Rim Countries. Thus the wider aspects of the Gujral doctrine recall the earlier dream of Jawaharlal Nehru for Asian and Afro-Asian cooperation, and the creation of an area of peace embracing all continents including the great powers in a global design of co-existence and cooperation. Although India's Foreign Policy during Gujral's tenure focussed primarily on its neighbours, it also established cordial relations with the international community at large. It also touched such fundamental issues as the creation of a nuclear-free world with complete and comprehensive nuclear disarmament. Shri Gujral as Prime Minister stood up to the pressures of the great powers on signing of the CTBT, while emphatically announcing the principled stand of India on nuclear non-proliferation and disarmament that did not discriminate between the nuclear haves and the have-nots. Shri Gujral's foreign policy sought friendship and cooperation with all nations on the basis of equality and shared responsibility for peace and prosperity in the world.

This volume of speeches and writings of Shri Gujral as the Foreign Minister and the Prime Minister of India at a crucial period of our history is a significant contribution to the understanding of India's foreign policy. It is apt that this book is entitled *Continuity and Change: India's Foreign Policy.* I pay my compliments to Shri Gujral for his creative reformulation of the essential tenets of India's foreign policy as conceived by Jawaharlal Nehru for the new and changing world of our times and congratulate Macmillan India Ltd. for bringing out this attractive volume.

KR Narayanan
New Delhi, 2002

Acknowledgements

Policy makers and practitioners of diplomacy in India remain indebted to the guiding star of Indian Foreign Policy, Jawaharlal Nehru who laid its firm foundation. His vision of world peace, Non-Alignment and good neighbourliness guided me to make my modest contribution which came to be known as 'The Gujral Doctrine'.

I am thankful to Shri VP Singh and Shri Deve Gowda, former Prime Ministers who gave me complete support when I served under them as Foreign Minister of India.

I would be failing in my duty if I do not thank Shri KR Narayanan who occupied the Rashtrapati Bhawan during my tenures as Foreign Minister and Prime Minister. He has made a distinct mark as an accomplished practitioner of diplomacy. I frequently drew on his rich experience.

My thanks to Shri AB Vajpayee who shared his views with me when he was adorning the opposition benches, he continues to do so while he strives for peace and goodwill as Prime Minister.

I am thankful to former Prime Minister Shri PV Narasimha Rao, whose deep understanding of the intricacies of Foreign Policy are widely recognized. He advised me on various occasions.

I heartily thank my friends, the experts in Foreign Affairs, Prof. Bhabani Sen Gupta, Prof. VP Dutt, Prof. SD Muni, Shri Pran Chopra, Shri N Ram and Shri Kuldip Nayar with whom I interacted from time to time to clarify my views.

xiii

I express my appreciation and thanks to Sarv Shri SK Singh, Muchkund Dubey, Salman Haider and K Raghunath who competently headed the Ministry of External Affairs as Foreign Secretaries during my tenures. If Indian diplomacy has matured and made its mark, it is primarily due to the fact that during the half century of its evolution the Foreign Service has produced men and women of admirable merit. I heartily thank them for their support.

In our scheme of things the Prime Minister's office plays a pivotal role in the country's diplomacy and this becomes all the more vital when the Prime Minister himself holds the charge of Foreign Affairs as happened in my case. In discharging the onerous tasks, I was assisted by two officials of outstanding merit—Shri TR Satish Chandran and Shri NN Vohra who had already made their mark as administrators. I am thankful to them for their advice.

I also highly appreciate the help and support rendered to me by Mr Avay Shukla, IAS, Mr AK Pandey, IFS, and Mr Bal Krishan Magoon. They made themselves available at all hours of the day even past midnight sometimes which made my task lighter during my various tenures.

Last but not the least, I heartily thank Mr Joseph Mathai and Ms Shuchi Srivastava of Macmillan, the publishers for bringing out this fine volume.

Contents

Prologue

This book is a companion volume to *A Foreign Policy for India*, which received the attention of scholars and practitioners of diplomacy. This book too stems from a long-felt desire to share my experiences, observations and assessments of the evolving world situation and India's responses to them at crucial times in our recent history.

Reflecting on my experiences over the years that I held charge of India's policies I remain more than convinced that the basic premises and approach were correct and the passage of time has amply demonstrated their soundness. Jawaharlal Nehru's vision had bequeathed to India the broad paradigms of our foreign policy. The task of his successors was to prudently inter-pret and correlate it to emerging scenarios. With this perspective I initiated the new policy framework that came to be known as the 'Gujral Doctrine' a fresh approach in international relations, not just towards our neighbours, but the world as a whole.

This approach rested on two premises. Firstly, that without genuine cooperation among nations no problem could be resolved and no real advance was feasible, and that prosperity of all countries depended on their working together towards better management of the scarce resources of the earth under a more equitable economic order. Secondly, the Gujral doctrine held that neighbouring countries could not change their geographical position and had the option of either living in perpetual animosity and conflict or alternatively striving to achieve

xvii

harmony and cooperation. The latter option would enable them to share the benefits of modern technology and uplift the living conditions of their people while the former would only perpetrate hatred and animus that in turn would accentuate misery and poverty.

A close study of the lessons of history convinced me that whenever necessary and required, India should be prepared to offer unilateral concessions to improve relationships with neighbouring countries. In doing so, there was no need to either sacrifice India's basic and vital interests or to compromise on its time-honoured principles. I was no starry-eyed idealist ignoring the element of reciprocity in international relations, but saw no contradiction in going an extra mile to inspire confidence and generate momentum towards building up new partnerships in South Asia. As may be seen, in pursuing such policies India achieved some unprecedented and durable successes. This approach of accommodation has proven more beneficial than a narrow-obsession with mechanical reciprocity.

In a similar vein, focused efforts were made to enlarge and intensify relations with South-East Asia, China, USA, Russia, Europe, Africa and others. Without animus or arrogance, but with self-confidence and dignity, that Mahatma Gandhi and Nehru had bestowed our nation with I strove to reach out to other countries and regions. We had no real quarrel with most of them. All that we desired was that these countries adopt positive policies to harmonize their interests with ours.

It fell to my lot to orient our foreign policy during the period of bewilderingly rapid changes wherein one kind of world was ushered out and another kind ushered in. The war against Iraq was one watershed and the fall of the Soviet Union another. Some confusion was sought to be created about India's standpoint on the Iraq-Kuwait war. Some overseas scribes tended to ignore the intense diplomatic effort that we engaged in during that period and forgot that situations had rapidly worsened, that the Soviet system had declined from within, that the attack by one Non-Aligned country on another was causing disarray among the NAM and the Revolution in Military Affairs (RMA) was drastically changing the power configuration in the world.

Under the circumstances it was our primary task to ensure the safety of nearly 200,000 of our follow citizens stuck in Iraq and Kuwait. The biggest aerial evacuation operation in recent history was successfully arranged; which has acquired a place in record books The operation was lauded by both Houses of Parliament. At the same time, we kept in step with UN resolutions and in keeping with their directions allowed the US forces to use our airspace.

The Iraq-Kuwait war coincided with the collapse of the mighty USSR. Never since the end of the British and other colonial empires had the world witnessed such a drastic realignment in global power parities. The Soviet Union was our strategic partner and a dependable friend. It was also our next door neighbour whose borders extended upto the Amur river. With its entry in to Afghanistan, its area of influence had extended across the Khyber Pass which had grave strategic implications for South Asia. The spectre and the consequences of that intrusion continue to haunt the region to this day. At the same time the world saw the emergence of the dominance of one power bloc. All this required a reorientation of policies to respond to the new challenges. It goes to the credit of our fundamental principles that we did not get disoriented and were able to quickly adapt to the new situation.

I came back to the foreign office in 1996 at the helm of our foreign policy after an interregnum of nearly 5 years. This time it was possible to pursue and work out my new framework in comparatively tranquil circumstances. The new state of Russia was struggling to stabilize its policy and to develop a new relationship with the United States, which had emerged as the world's sole super power.

The 'New World Order' was no more equitable than the one preceding it. It sought to make permanent the hegemony of the five permanent members of the UN Security Council (all nuclear powers). The most obvious example of this was the attempt to perpetuate the nuclear monopoly of these powers through the NPT and the CTBT. In unison they were pressurizing India to sign the CTBT, a flawed treaty that was neither comprehensive nor fair. It placed one-sided obligations on the non-nuclear countries and gave equally one-sided advantages to those designated as nuclear powers. There was no way I could agree to the signing away of India's autonomy on such a vital issue.

Since the days of Nehru, every Government in India had pleaded unsuccessfully with the big powers to work towards elimination of weapons of mass destruction under a verifiable supervisory mechanism and rid the world of the nuclear Damocles Sword hanging over humanity's head, but the nuclear powers were unwilling to forego their own monopoly and control of such awesome destructive power. Yet, they demanded that the threshold powers give up their nuclear research and development even while they themselves tried to secure the sanction of the international community to continue augmenting their capability of precision bombing.

India had desisted after the 1974 test, from conducting any further sub-soil blast but had to refuse to sign the CTBT, a treaty that did not aim at nuclear disarmament and could only be regarded as a ploy to sustain the monopoly of the P-5 and to enable them to continue upgrading the refinement, sophistication and lethality of their nuclear weapons. If the possession of nuclear weapons did not confer on a country any special role or any special advantages, why were the P-5 meeting again and again to lay down the law in the nuclear field for everyone else?

I had told President Clinton that India being surrounded by an arc of nuclear weapons, extending from Diego Garcia to the Gulf and Pakistan and China, could not for long remain oblivious to these realities and the security concerns that they aroused. In the years after I demitted office India became a declared nuclear weapons power with all its implications and consequences. This was both foreseeable and unavoidable. In my own way and with utmost politeness, I had hinted at this possibility to President Bill Clinton and Jacques Chirac during my meetings with them.

Yet a world order based on the possession of such horrendous weapons by a few must remain a fragile one. A small spark could set a blazing fire across the world that could consume human civilization itself. The risk element is just too great for anyone's comfort and India must therefore, remain focused on the central requirement: comprehensive nuclear disarmament under international supervision.

To rid the world of this monstrous menace and to make our voice heard more effectively, it would be highly useful if India and Pakistan were to resolve their tensions and work towards a more purposeful and constructive relationship, just as it is equally necessary that India and China should raise the level and intensity of their interaction and strive for qualitatively better relations.

We are all living under the shadow of terrorism and the fight against it has become the rallying point for the international community. If the subcontinent could rid itself of this phenomenon, the countries of the region could take urgently needed measures for reducing poverty and improving the well-being of the people, which in the final analysis is the only real guarantee for peace and security.

India has been able to keep its head above the water despite all the storms in the international relations, because it has remained faithful to its basic principles and because it has continued to follow a sober and judicious foreign policy. This capacity to combine change with continuity has been our strength in foreign policy areas. We have remained true to our basic commitments and have simultaneously given them a healthy realistic foundation of national interests, amidst the changing equations of international power politics.

New Delhi   IK GUJRAL
August 2002

I

THE FUNDAMENTAL
PRINCIPLES

1

India's Fifty Years: Achievements, Promises and Challenges*

In 1997 we celebrated the Golden Jubilee Year of our freedom. This was also an occasion for the 960 million people of our country to take stock of the situation, to look forward to a future while at the same time draw strength from its past. Our attempt was to articulate a vision for the twenty-first century in conformity with our needs and potential. The Parliament of India met in a Special Session, where in an unprecedented move that rose above the din of familiar debate and party affiliations, both Houses participated in an in-depth analysis of the country's achievements and shortcomings. The essence of what emerged from this effort was a collective reaffirmation of the nation's commitment to democracy, economic growth and social equity and a peaceful world free of nuclear weapons.

When reflecting upon our achievements, the first thing that comes to my mind is that, in all these years since 1947, India has not only survived but flourished as a democracy.

---

* Collated from speeches delivered at the Council of Foreign Relations, New York 3/10/1996, the Asia Society, New York, 23/9/1997 and the National Defence College, 13/11/1997.

Broadest Representative Base

Millions of Indians may still be unlettered and inadequately fed and sheltered, but they have enthusiastically participated in ensuring that democracy takes deep roots in our soil. In the last 50 years, 11 polls to Parliament have taken place. The elections have been scrupulously fair and largely peaceful. The percentage of those voting has been higher than in many other long-standing democracies. A great number of political parties both at the regional and national level have had the freedom to represent the widest range of opinion across the democratic spectrum. The size of the electorate has grown steadily.

It is interesting to note that all political parties, both in the opposition and in the government, had decided that 30 per cent of seats in Parliament from the next session onwards would be reserved for women. And we are still called a backward society! I would like to know which other country was willing to offer 30 per cent—one-third of its seats in Legislative Assemblies to women. Equally interesting was when the bill was brought in the Parliament, the consensus was 'don't debate it, pass it', because we all wanted it. It was with great difficulty that we persuaded everybody to let it go to the select committee because certain issues had to be sorted out. It was also decided by Constitutional Amendment that in all rural and district areas, district councils and Panchayats, 30 per cent membership must be of women. There are now many villages and numerous councils headed by women. And very often we came across a story in the paper where a totally illiterate woman has come to head the council and yet delivers the goods.

A notable feature, which may perhaps be a revelation to some, is the institutional strength of democracy in our country at the grassroots levels. As of 1997, starting from the village upwards, there were nearly 2,50,000 democratically-elected local bodies or Panchayats manned by over 3 million elected repre-

4

sentatives, who together constituted one of the broadest representative base to exist in any country of the world.

An important aspect of the Indian democratic resilience is the ability to adapt and accommodate to changing realities. If, in the past, India had seen the preponderance of a single dominant party, namely the Congress, then, of late the Indian people have also used their democratic prerogative to mandate a coalition government in New Delhi. When this happened, many observers at home and abroad jumped to the conclusion that India was on the brink of instability and would soon become ungovernable. However, the great democratic experiment in India has had a tendency to confound the Doubting Thomases. Politics when moulded by a genuinely democratic system, accurately reflects the new ground realities. I have had the honour of heading a government that is distinguished by the direct participation of 13 political parties spanning the entire country. These political parties, some national, others regional, covered the largest segment of the political spectrum and significantly rectified the earlier imbalance in representation between the north and the south of the country. Thus, around the cabinet table we had a far more authentic representation of aspirations from all parts of the country. It is true that this very aspect of enhanced participation sometimes also required greater coordination. The country was seeking to respect the mandate of the people by fine-tuning the methodology and culture of a coalition form of government.

Population Problems

The growing population was a matter of concern; family planning movements had been going on for a long time. But we had been multiplying all the same. We are now a country of over a billion people. Experience has taught us that posters, propaganda, films, etc., don't solve the problem; it is how fast and how many people we can conduct into what I choose to call the standard of living circuit. This is the only line that is available to contain the population. In 40 per cent or so of the Indian population, which constitutes the emerging market, the family consists of one or two children. But once we consider the remaining 60 per cent, we are confronted with a problem. I think this problem is totally associated with and is the outcome of poverty. Therefore, poverty amelioration programmes are bound to have an impact on both family composition and family size. In the Ministry of Information, we tried all sorts of propaganda but it did not bring about desired results. We coined very beautiful slogans but it only kept converting the already converted. It did not percolate down the line and that is why we came to the conclusion that we should concentrate on three things: poverty amelioration programmes, education of women and mass literacy programmes. If these three move forward, probably population can be managed.

Largest Reservoir of Manpower

One of our significant achievements is that India is perhaps one of the few recently independent countries where democracy and economic growth have not been at the cost of one or the other. It is true that certain economic goals can perhaps be achieved faster and more effectively provided the right to dissent and the freedom of expression are curtailed. Many countries have been unable to resist such a temptation but in India, the democratic spirit has always prevailed even if sometimes it has created, in the short term, its own frustrations as regards the pace and speed of change. There is no doubt that we in India have still to do a great deal in the areas of poverty eradication, illiteracy and basic health care among other priorities. But it is also true that a great deal has been achieved in the last 50 years and that too peacefully and within a democratic framework. In the field of agriculture, from a country dependent on food im-

6

ports to feed its people, India has become, thanks in large measure to the Green Revolution initiated in the 1960s, a net exporter of foodgrains. In 1997, our foodgrains output stood close to 200 million tons and we possessed a grain reserve of 21 million tons. Over the years, we have built up a diverse industrial infrastructure and one of the world's largest reservoirs of skilled and trained manpower. I recall that, in 1947, even a sewing needle had to be imported. Today, manufactured products are a vital segment of our export basket. Our scientists have done our country proud in the frontier areas of space, ocean technology, biotechnology and meteorology and Indians are breaking new ground in the areas of electronics, in particular, software development.

Sustained Economic Growth

In a democracy, economic reforms are an exercise in political persuasion and management and yet, our direction remains clear as also our determination to deepen the reform process. In the last three years, the economic growth has averaged 7 per cent per year and if we are able to sustain this growth for the next decade, we will greatly succeed in abolishing poverty, in India, which must remain the overriding objective of our reforms.

Commensurate with our priorities, my Government was committed to further deregulating and opening up the economy. The rupee was stable in a sea of turbulence and full convertibility was on the horizon. Inflation was below 4 per cent annually. Foreign currency reserves were comfortable. Foreign investment flows were rising and we believed that we would be able to absorb as much as US$10 billion annually. The Bombay Stock Exchange has the largest number of listed companies in the world. Our annual output of scientific and technological manpower is close to a quarter of a million and the country is brimming with entrepreneurial skills.

There is a developing consensus among economists that South Asia is potentially a region where growth rates will be the fastest in the next 30 years. It is estimated that India will emerge as the fourth largest economy in the world by the year 2015, and one of the largest markets in the world with the middle class estimated to be around 500 million by the year 2025.

The Kashmir Situation

As far as Kashmir is concerned, a major turning point was the conducting of elections for the Parliament and the State Assembly in 1996. The elections were free and fair. In the given circumstances, certain difficulties were inevitable, because people had to come to vote under the shadow of violence. One policy decision that we took at the central level was that we would not try to form a coalition of parties in Kashmir. We wanted every party to fight independently. Even those parties who were participating in the Central Government preferred to go it alone. Therefore, they managed 5–7 seats, but that did not bother us. The main idea was, and continues to be, not the number of seats one wins, but to give Kashmir free and fair elections, which was very important in view of past performances. So far as the autonomy issue was concerned, the Government of India stood committed to the fact that once the Government of Kashmir was formed, talks would be held to discuss various dimensions of autonomy that they were thinking of.

Triumph of Unity Despite Adversities

In fact, an important aspect, which I believe should figure in any balance sheet that we draw up as we look back over the last five decades, is that the unity of India has triumphed over all the challenges, covert or overt, that have been directed against it. I myself recall that there were several distinguished observers in

8

1947, and even later, who felt that the unity of India was an artificial construct, an incidental consequence of unintended British benevolence and that, with progress and development and increased aspirations and expectations, this unity would be overwhelmed by the country's myriad diversities. I am glad to say that such a prognosis has been proved to be dramatically wrong. With economic growth and political maturity, the diversities of India have found greater expression. But this very assertiveness is a tribute to the success of the democratic process and its ability to absorb different pulls and pressures to harmonize newly empowered sections and often competing demands. This results in an increase in the quality and range of a country's representativeness and in the process, revitalizes its essential unity. The fact that many regional parties are now represented in the central government indicates the strength of our democratic policy. There is definite attraction about the Great Indian Enterprise that channelizes the numerous tributaries that binds all its people into one essential mainstream. It was about this indefinable but essential sense of oneness that the great poet-patriot, Subramaniam Bharati spoke when he said:

She has three hundred million faces
But one sole life, majestic and strong
Eighteen are her tongues for utterance
And yet, her heart is one

A vital factor underpinning this unity is that India has remained and will remain a secular State. In terms of religion, the Hindus may constitute the majority in our country, but the founding fathers of the nation, Mahatma Gandhi and Jawaharlal Nehru, and other stalwarts of the freedom movement, had decided much before our independence that India must remain a land where all religions have freedom of faith and worship. The basic premise was that once we accept that nationality is founded upon religion, we break up the whole concept of India. It is a matter of pride that India has the second largest number of Muslims in the world and all the major religions have their followers in our country.

My euphoria at some of the achievements of our country may be pardoned, but my faith and pride are born out of personal experience. Fifty years ago, my wife and I arrived in New Delhi as refugees from Pakistan. Fifty years later, I had the honour of being the Prime Minister of this very country. This is the miracle of India, a miracle that has also made it possible to elect as the President of the Republic, Mr KR Narayanan, a distinguished scholar, diplomat and statesman, who, as a member of one of the most oppressed social categories of our country, had to struggle against the severest odds to even complete his education.

Today, we stand on the threshold of the new millennium. My countrymen and I have a vision for the future and following are some of the elements that constitute it:

Freedom of Thought and Action

One of the fundamental principles that India's foreign policy has always sought to uphold and will continue to uphold is to fully preserve the freedom of independent thought and action. I know we have been accused by some to be more willing to 'preach' than to 'practice' and to unproductively prefer ideology to expediency. The fact of the matter is that a country is a product of its own history and experience. The way it behaves is moulded by the way it came into being. A nation with a 5000-year-old history and culture cannot suddenly reincarnate itself as a pliable echo of somebody else's expectations. Our freedom was the result of one of the most profoundly ethical and visionary struggles that history has witnessed and the principles of our

10

foreign policy cannot but be influenced by that experience. Our desire to remain Non-Aligned was not an attempt to carve out a platform of manoeuvrability and leverage for ourselves but to extend our hard won freedom to the arena of international diplomacy.

A Full Dialogue Partner

With this as background, the vision of our foreign policy is rooted in our geographical position in South Asia, our initiatives vis-à-vis our immediate neighbours, as a major presence in the Indian Ocean and as a close and concerned neighbour of the Gulf region and Central Asia. Jawaharlal Nehru voiced India's potential 50 years ago when he said that India is so situated that she is the pivot of western, southern and South-East Asia. We sought to cement the commonalties and complementarities within South Asia, to strengthen our status as a Full Dialogue Partner (FDP) with the Association of South-East Asian Nations (ASEAN) nations, to forge greater cooperation among the Indian Ocean Rim (IOR) countries, to find new ways to increase cooperation for mutual benefit with the Gulf nations, to reinforce our civilizational linkages to Central Asia and to achieve greater understanding with developed nations.

If strength in the modern world today means economic growth, the ASEAN is definitely a remarkable identity. When the South Asian Association for Regional Cooperation (SAARC) as an institution grows further, our neighbourhood market would be larger which we definitely want to encourage. As a matter of fact, when I was in Bangladesh, one of the issues that we discussed at length was the host country's interest in foreign investments which would be difficult to come by if the Indian market provided stiff competition. We agreed not to stand in their way, and our entire approach and outlook was that sooner rather than later, a stage would come when ASEAN investments would

11

collectively benefit the entire region. Upon being asked by a journalist as to how I would react to Pakistan joining the ASEAN, I replied that the matter was between ASEAN and Pakistan and India would not interfere. This was our general outlook. We were looking forward to collaboration with the ASEAN and its investment in any country in the region.

India and SAARC

In the South Asian region, we have taken significant steps to implement this vision and we remain optimistic on the move in SAARC from the South Asian Preferential Trade Agreement (SAPTA) to the South Asian Free Trade Agreement (SAFTA). We are aware that India is the largest country in South Asia. The population of other South Asian countries put together is less than half of that of India and India's GNP is more than twice that of the combined GNP of some its South Asian neighbours. But we do not see our size and strength as an instrument for dominating the region for the simple reason that we consider it to be in our interest to improve relations with our neighbours. Consequently, we consciously chose to pursue an asymmetrical policy. In simple terms, this means that while dealing with our neighbours, we are willing to do more for them than they can do for us. Such a policy, which some people have called the Gujral Doctrine, is based on certain principles that require mutual understanding and agreement. It asks that relations be founded on good faith and trust; that no country allows its territory to be used against the interests of another country in the region; that none interfere in the internal affairs of another; that all respect each other's territorial integrity and sovereignty; and; that disputes be solved through peaceful bilateral negotiations.

I am happy to say that such an approach, which at least for India is not strictly based on a mechanical calculation of cost and benefit, has paid rich dividends and did lead to a significant strengthening of the atmosphere of trust and cooperation with some of our neighbours.

With Nepal, India's relationship has remained traditional. There is an open order between the two countries. After the United Front Government came into office, we extended it further. Major concessions were given in trade and, particularly on the concept of country of origin. We also gave Bangladesh a direct transit route through Indian territory to Nepal. We were trying to forge new types of tranquil relationships. The Parliament in Nepal also approved the Mahakali Treaty, which was signed by the governments of India and Nepal. In the Nepali Constitution, it was important that a two-third majority must endorse any international treaty, which it did, thereby enhancing our relationship. With Myanmar, we have traditionally shared a good relationship. With Sri Lanka also we have developed a good bilateral relationship. Unfortunately, their own internal problems troubled them but India's foreign policy continued to be that of non-intervention in their internal affairs. There were reports of arms being supplied to the Tamil Tigers from Tamil Nadu. Unfortunately, it so happens that arms bazaars are autonomous zones. But fortunately, the arms bazaars in India are extremely limited and well under control. The Government of India has never encouraged any arms supply to militants. We wanted Sri Lanka to stabilize and were strongly opposed to its dismemberment. Thus, whatever problems Sri Lanka faced, we retained our policy of non-interference, either directly or by implication. We did our utmost to give a new turn to Indo-Pak relations. There had not been any single occasion during my tenure as Prime Minister when the Government of India issued any inflammatory statements about Pakistan. We refused to react even to provocative statements. Unilaterally, we took several steps regarding issuing visas and posting of journalists in India. A change in the government in Pakistan put paid to that positive development.

13

Sino-Indian Relations

So far as Sino-India relations are concerned, we have an outstanding problem on the border, which the Joint Working Group had been working to resolve. Despite this, it was very encouraging for us to see that our trade was growing as were our interactions. On the whole, the relationship between India and China was on an upswing. I would not say that we had solved all our problems but can safely admit that we were definitely moving in that direction.

Indo-Myanmar Relations

We share borders with Myanmar. We empathize with the agony that the Myanmar people are going through on the issue of democracy. As a policy, the Government of India does not believe in import and export of ideologies and more so of democracy. Ultimately, every society has to carve its own polity. Our sympathy lies with democratic societies but as a government, we do not approve of direct interference. The more important question for us to consider is who is helping Myanmar's military regime? Although the United States does not approve of the military regime in Myanmar, multinational companies based in the US take advantage of the economic concessions offered by the Myanmar Government to invest in the country. There is a strange dichotomy which is really not allowing the democratic movement in Myanmar to gain momentum. China's interest in that country is obvious as it has invested a lot in the country. We had information that China had given Myanmar arms supplies worth $ 4 billion.

Indo-Russian Relations

Russia has always been our neighbour. When it was the Soviet

Union, our borders were closer. That reality in geo-strategic terms has not ceased but continues. Russia has contributed tremendously to the building of India's infrastructure, both industrial and defence. Indo-Russian relationship should be given very high priority while undertaking foreign policy decisions.

Indo-US Relationship

The Indo-American relationship has always been very distinct. We have great regard for America. It continues to be the largest trade partner of India, and also the largest investor. On various others issues also we are cooperating and collaborating. To maintain friendly relations with the US continues to be one of the primary goals of the Indian foreign policy. There were sharp differences of opinion regarding the Comprehensive Test Ban Treaty (CTBT). However, it's the strength of the Indo-American relationship, that despite differences on one issue we continue to collaborate on others.

A World Free from Nuclear Weapons

An essential part of our vision was the creation of a nuclear weapons-free world and we hoped that it would become a reality in the near future. The truth is that India was among the first countries since the 1950s to advance the cause of a nuclear weapons-free world. We have consistently demanded the halting of all nuclear tests. We welcomed the Partial Test Ban Treaty as a first step towards a comprehensive ban on underground tests. For us, a nuclear weapons-free planet is an article of faith and so we called for a global elimination of all nuclear weapons within a time-bound framework. India did not sign the nuclear Non-Proliferation Treaty (NPT) because of its inherent flaws, which legitimize the possession of nuclear weapons by a few countries while denying them to others. When the question of

15

the Comprehensive Test Ban Treaty (CTBT) was being discussed, we made it clear that we would not accept the draft unless it contained a pledge by the nuclear powers that they would proceed towards complete nuclear disarmament within a reasonable time frame. Our views did not get any response, leaving us with no option but to decline from signing the treaty.

India was, of course, dubbed unreasonable, but in matters where both our interests and principles were concerned, we had to uphold our point of view. I am reminded, in this context, of a rather pertinent remark by George Bernard Shaw: The reasonable man adapts himself to the world, the unreasonable one persists in trying to adapt the world to himself. Therefore, all progress depends on the unreasonable man.

We are surrounded by nuclear weapons. In the East, there is China, a full-fledged nuclear power. In the South, there is Diego Garcia, a major American nuclear base. In the West, the Gulf region has been nuclearized by alien powers. And in the North, the world is aware of Pakistan's nuclear weapons programme which led the former President Bush to withhold certification. Indian security concerns should therefore be understandable. We cannot give up our nuclear option unless the world around us is made nuclear weapons-free.

A New World Order

As the largest democracy in the world as also a factor for peace and stability in our region and beyond, India will continue to play an active role in the more effective functioning of the United Nations. We believe that in the efforts for the creation of a New World Order supported by the twin pillars of peace and equity, the UN must continue to play an effective and pivotal role. Our support for the reform of the UN, to make it a more democratic body and more representative of the aspirations of the developing countries stems from this premise. We have been constructively engaged in a dialogue with other countries on the question of the expansion of the Security Council. It is our conviction that on the basis of any global, non-discriminatory and objective criteria such as the size of the economy, population, support to the principles of the UN Charter including its peace-keeping operations, and future potential, India's case for a permanent membership of the expanded UN Security Council is self-evident.

I had once the occasion to go through the report of the study mission sponsored by the Asian Society on the subject of 'South Asia and the United States after the Cold War'. I was encouraged to note that the report recommended that economic relations would be the focal point of US engagement with the South Asian region. There are immense opportunities in such an approach for both countries. The US is India's largest trade partner and the biggest source of Foreign Direct Investment (FDI). If our huge emerging market, a strong institutional and legal framework, a professional and entrepreneurial class, and scientific and technical skills are an attraction for the US, the US too needs to be a more easily accessible market for India's exports and a source for required technology. The basis for an expanding and mutually beneficial interaction is there and both countries need to seize the existing opportunities.

We ask the US and its people to participate in the Great Indian Enterprise. The world's oldest and largest democracies have a common sense of inspiration: democracy, rule of law, tolerance, equality and non-discrimination coupled with myriad diversities within our respective systems. We strongly believe that these very principles should form the basis of an international order for the future. We remain ready to go that extra mile, to take that extra step and concretize such a world order that would be just, equitable, humane, non-discriminatory and democratic. These ideals had inspired Mahatma Gandhi, they imbue the Indian Constitution and they give us the strength to continue into this new century with faith and courage.

The twenty-first century is the age of globalization. The challenge will be to ensure that a globalized economy also creates a global community on the principles of equality. Global interdependence has to be matched by a respect for sovereignty. An increasingly common global destiny has to accommodate human diversity and plurality. The information revolution needs to be balanced by the key issues of ethics and access. We have to ensure that vital technologies do not become new instruments for perpetuating inequality amongst nations. The preservation of the environment of our planet has to be a common goal for every nation. But we have to share the burden equitably and not place an unfair responsibility on only a few. We have to take care to see that issues of human rights and democracy are tackled in a spirit of cooperation and not used as a means for perpetuating old divides through new conditions. We have to evolve a global view of security, and learn to jointly tackle the menace of drug trafficking, terrorism and cross-border crimes. Most importantly, we have to work to reduce economic disparities across the world, between the rich and the poor. This, perhaps, will be the biggest challenge facing the global community, as there can be no lasting peace in the world if the institutional global systems that control the flow of wealth and technology remain insensitive to the needs and demands of the vast majority of the poor and impoverished. India has been in the forefront when it comes to championing the cause of developing countries and will continue to ensure that the voices and concerns of developing countries are heard and properly addressed.

I have touched upon some issues of foreign policy that constitute an integral part of our vision for the future. I see an India on the move, proud of its democratic traditions, secure in its unity and seeking to build a new superstructure on the strong economic foundations laid thus far. I envision an India striving to forge ahead on the basis of institutions which are established beyond doubt: the rule of law, a vigilant media, a free judiciary

18

and an executive and legislature accountable to the will of the people. I visualize an India that is changing because its people want change and a better quality of life within their lifetime, an India which will strive for social equity and education for all, the growth of its infrastructure, planned regional development, gender justice and the creation of a scientific temperament.

2

Historical Roots of the
Indian Foreign Policy*

The world was always present in the philosophies of India; our mythologies and folklores bear witness to this fact. Though the apertures of our vision varied with time, our world view was remarkably sensitive and intellectual.

Alexander's invasion made us look westward to discover a world beyond Iran. Europe to us became a political reality. Our civilizational interactions till then were directed towards the South-East and East Asia. Thailand, Vietnam, Indonesia, Cambodia and other countries of the east still exhibit the fingerprints of those eras.

The *zamorins* of Calicut were the first in the subcontinent to see the European invasions coming from across the seas. But their formidable naval strength fought and pushed the Portuguese back. For a good part of the fifteenth century, the Portuguese tried to gain a foothold into the subcontinent several times but were routed by the valiant *zamorins*. If their marine technology had been steam based, the *zamorins* would have pursued them beyond the Straits of Hormuz. But it was not to be. The Portuguese recouped and regrouped in the Gulf to attack

---

*Speech delivered at the India International Centre, 1996.

again. With this began an era that ended with four centuries of the European colonization of Asia.

The Ganga-Jamuna Civilization

Stories of the journeys along the fabulous silk route and the memories of Ibn-Batuta and Hsuen Tsang tell us how India was transacting both commercially and culturally with the then known world. In the process, new philosophies and languages were born. Buddha's message thus reached beyond the seas and the Himalayas. There is no phase in Indian history when Indians did not interact with the rest of the world.

We transacted with the incoming waves of cultures, ideas, religions and the metaphysical perceptions. We transmitted our philosophies and absorbed whatever would suit us. Nehru often reminded us of the assimilating capability of the Indian civilization. The message of Buddha traveled across the width of Central Asia, Tibet and China and touched the borders of Europe. India always met the world in a two-way street. It was never a one-way journey. This process of dynamic interaction continues even when we are inducting new technologies from abroad and our 'software' capabilities now are highly rated by the West.

I am reminded of Nehru's *Discovery of India,* where confined to the narrow jail cells, he looked at the Indian ethos and its dynamics that were intimately related to the world that enriched our culture till the colonial era distorted the civilizational unity of the subcontinent. The historic relationships built over the centuries with the north and the east were obstructed by the alien rulers yet our resilience withstood it to emerge again after our Independence.

Assimilation and Defiance

If I were to sum up the long history of our cultural journey, I

21

would spell it in two words: Assimilation and Defiance. We assimilated new technologies, new ideas and new languages. At the same time, we did not get overwhelmed by them. The articulation of the defiance took several forms in our literatures and is the unique character of our freedom struggle.

I am reminded of Raja Rammohan Roy and his contribution towards modernization of India. He urged us to benefit from the western sciences and European thoughts while sustaining our Indianness. Tagore had a similar message. Gurudev made us look at the world in a way that would open us to the world. Gandhi and Tagore had identical outlooks in several matters. Their articulations were distinct yet they were constantly updating our thoughts and outlooks. In their unique ways, they brought the world to India and took India to the world. Tagore's writings won him international acclaim in the form of the Nobel prize. Gandhi asked us to keep our 'windows open'. He did not want us to shut ourselves to new ideas, that the post-Renaissance west was projecting. At the same time, he wanted us to stay firm with our cultural ethics.

Ghare Baire (Home and the World)

During the colonial era, our nationalism intensified the anti-imperialist emotions. But even then we are not exclusivists. Exclusivity was resisted by Gurudev Tagore. I am reminded of his famous novel *Ghare Baire,* where Gurudev said: 'You must not let yourself drown in blind nationalism. Humanism and nationalism need not be intra-contradictory. They must coexist.' Humanism was the message that he sent all the time. From Tagore to Gandhi, we received the same message.

When Gandhi started Satyagraha, he gave us new ideas and also familiarized us with the world of Africa. This region that was helplessly and hopelessly struggling against the colonizers found a powerful voice in Gandhi. As Nelson Mandela once

22

said, 'Though Gandhi was physically born in India but politically he took birth in South Africa.' His Satyagraha forged an invisible link between the people of the two continents and added another dimension to our world view. Gandhi introduced us to the turmoil of the African people. Through him, we discovered that the tormented world was much larger and more intensely exploited by the colonizers. Via Gandhi again, we committed ourselves to their cause. Nehru expanded our dimensions. I recall cynical reactions when Nehru deputed a medical mission to Spain during the anti-fascist war. Confronting such cynicism is a part of a leader's fate. We all face such reactions when new initiatives are taken or new policies projected. Nehru's medical mission to Spain during the civil war was a message of solidarity with the victims of Nazism and Fascism. Similar was the purpose of the mission led by Dr Kotnis to China. Dr Kotnis, as you know, died in the far lands of Yunnan serving the people of China. His sacrifice thus cemented relations between the two countries.

I recall my meeting with Dr Kotnis prior to his departure for China. He came to Lahore to address a large gathering but he did not know Hindi or Punjabi. I was an undergraduate student. It fell to my lot to interpret him. For me it continues to be a memorable experience. I witnessed a new vision that Nehru was projecting through Dr Kotnis. Nehru had visited the USSR in the middle of the 1920s. His writings familiarized us with a new social order there, since the British rulers had barred our interactions with countries beyond Afghanistan. Nehru's writings enabled the country to see and judge events in the neighbouring countries. The USSR had made an appeal on behalf of our freedom struggle. Even in the midst of our freedom struggle that had incarcerated him several times, Nehru educated the country about the world. That is how Nehru constructed the foreign policies for the future. India, he rightly believed, could never be alone or neutral. A vast country with a rich history and tradition

23

could never be neutral in any struggle between the oppressor and the oppressed. India continues to be on the side of those who are exploited or enslaved by the colour discriminators. Fascist regimes were abnormal to this way of thinking.

I am reminded of Gurudev Tagore's anguish-ridden poem when China was attacked. He wrote:

The marching armies plant flags on the ashes of desolate homes, desecrate the centres of culture and shrines of beauty, mark red with blood their trail across green meadows and populace and markets and so they march to the temple of Buddha, the compassionate with loud beats of drums rat-a-tat and earth trembles.

Gurudev thus articulated the soul of India that was echoed by Gandhi too. One was lyrical, the other was earthy but there was a communion of ideas.

Our World View

As we journeyed through to 15 August 1947, our world view became clearer. We chose to stand with those who were still victims of colonization. We stood with those who were victims of colour discrimination. We were with the oppressed and with the movements for peace. Therefore, the outlines of our international relationships were already drawn by the time we became free. The chapter of the Indian foreign policy was not written by Nehru after becoming the Prime Minister; the freedom struggle itself had authored it.

In 1946, months before the Independence Day, Nehru as Deputy Chairman of the Viceroy's Executive Council convened the First Asia Conference in Delhi. Besides, Gandhi and Nehru,

24

a galaxy of Indian leaders participated in the event to give a resonant message that the freedom of India would be complete only when all the remnants of colonialism would vanish. We take pride that in these 50 years, we have never faltered. Every successive government in India has honoured this promise. The decolonization of the three continents was our cause, so was our support to the cause of Nelson Mandela and all the coloured people in South Africa. In matters of world peace, we continue to have a vested interest. India will continue to advocate and fight for all such noble causes that we hold dear since they conform with the paradigms of our freedom struggle.

Our concern for justice made us raise our voice against the invasion of Vietnam. Similarly, we did not hesitate in stating our views regarding the interventions in Korea. Our foreign policy always had a purpose—we would not align ourselves with the invaders, colonizers, dictators or war mongers.

As was inevitable, sometimes we had to pay a heavy price for these principled stands. We were denigrated and ridiculed. Yet, we stood by our principles. This has made us a proud nation. We take pride in our legacy that provides courage to defy and uphold our independent foreign policies. This has been maintained despite all pressures and in all circumstances.

Gandhian Outlook

Every foreign policy has to have both a short-term and long-term purpose. Gandhi had spelt the guidelines for our Indian diplomacy: to transform and to never compromise on the basics. This has been our mantra and we have never compromised on this. We always sought to transform an old world order for the benefit of the world as a whole. If you ask me to explain in one sentence where the Indian international relations have succeeded in the past 50 years, I would say we have succeeded in transforming the world's outlook and also in defeating the

25

colonizers. The liberation of South Africa from the Apartheid regime is one such success story that I could point out. When the British withdrew from Hong Kong, I sent one of my cabinet colleagues to represent India on the joyous occasion. We had two invitations, one from the British and the other from the Chinese. We responded to the Chinese invitation. The reason was simple. On the day of the liquidation of the last bastion of colonialism, I wanted my minister to sit with the Chinese and not on the imperialist's side.

You would recall that it was the East India Company that had imposed the opium wars on China to subjugate Hong Kong and Macao. The East India Company was cultivating poppy in India, to export opium to China and encourage opium addiction there—banning of the import of opium resulted in wars and subsequent colonization. Those who now worry about the tragic impact of drugs may recall how abhorrent were the ones who exported drugs initially. Who were the once destroying the morale of an entire nation? The Opium Wars ended in a century-long colonization of Hong Kong. Therefore, when Hong Kong was decolonized, we rejoiced because in a way we were fulfilling the promise that the Asia Conference had made to the world. India had said, 'Our freedom would not be complete till all colonies were liberated' and this has now happened. We continue to labour to change the world in favour of the poor and the oppressed.

This agenda made India an integral part of the developing world whose economies were exploited by the Imperial powers in the preceeding centuries. This was the motivation for Jawaharlal Nehru to author the Non-Alignment movement. NAM was never structured as a camp of the neutrals. It was an expression of the camaraderie that naturally existed between the victims of the colonizers who were politically and economically enslaved. Therefore, we got together to demand a fair deal for all of us. As in the past, the Indian Foreign Policy will not compromise on these

26

basics and will continue to derive strength from its legacy. Non-Alignment gave courage to the meek and surrounded them with a friendly fellowship. The NAM was befriended by the Soviet Union, whose perspective was acceptable to the Third World, primarily because of its helpful economic policies.

I had the privilege of serving as India's Ambassador to the USSR for nearly five years, which enabled me to understand the anatomy of the Indo-Soviet relations. As we all know, the base of heavy industry in India was built because of the Soviet cooperation. Let us also not forget that the innovation of 'rupee trade' was devised to help us when we didn't have any hard currency exchange reserves. In 1947, our national reserves were to the order of about Rs 200 crore. With this meagre capital, we ventured to build the nation's economy. Nehru was a great dreamer. He dreamt of India's greatness and its massive modern industrial base. Where would he look for support? The Soviet Union extended its helping hand when the erstwhile colonial powers were keen to keep us confined to the dungeons of backwardness. It appreciated our courageous and independent world view and helped us to build our economy. If today we have a massive industrial base, it is to a large extent due to the Soviet assistance. Despite all that has now happened to Russia, our foreign policy sustains a spirit of friendship with all countries that were once a part of the Soviet Union. This is an abiding friendship that has stood the test of time and we continued to assist Russia and the Central Asian States in their period of transition.

Courage to Defy

Gandhian Satyagraha was not for the feeble hearted but for the courageous. Gandhi taught us to stand up boldly and face the tyrants. This continues to be the spirit of the Indian foreign policy. The Cold War had divided neighbours since the allied powers

27

formed camps to encircle the USSR. India could not remain in any camp and have pre-determined foreign relations. The Indian political ethos would not look at the world in terms of the pros and the antis. We were for peace and universal friendships. This was an arduous task, especially since our neighbour Pakistan would not opt for an independent foreign policy. Under pressure from erstwhile imperialists, it was indulging in formenting tensions into the region. Nehru had repeatedly said that the tensions were being imported and imposed from outside. Since national security was our prime priority, we were forced to expand our arms inventories and divert resources towards the modernisation of the armed forces. But for these factors our economic policies would have been more dynamic.

I recall Jawaharlal Nehru saying in the Parliament on 3 February 1950, 'India and Pakistan, situated as they are geographically and otherwise and with their historical background, cannot carry on for ever as enemies. Millions of people live next door to one another and some time or other, those millions will have to come together. Will have to cooperate.' I endorse this as the spirit of our foreign policy.

New Challenges

For a realistic safeguarding of the nation's interest, every foreign policy must periodically reassess itself. Sometimes this forces a nation to temporarily deviate from its chosen path. Thanks to our resilient diplomacy, India has safeguarded its security without compromising on its basic principles. In the contemporary context, we have not relented from our stand regarding the Comprehensive Test Ban Treaty (CTBT). The Cold War has ended. India is presently confronted with new challenges and also new opportunities. In terms of foreign policy, globalization is important and so are regional relations. I focused a great deal on reorienting our relations with our immediate neighbours in the

SAARC, included the Indian Ocean Rim countries. A new chapter has been added by India joining the ASEAN as a full dialogue partner and co-authorizing the BITMC (Bangladesh, India, Thailand, Myanmar and China) cooperation.

As one is aware, the five nuclear powers have been making their weapons more sophisticated and target oriented. These are tested with the help of computers and simulators to avoid the letter of the CTBT. The CTBT—as I have often said—is a charade. It is neither comprehensive nor does it ban all types of tests. It seeks to ban only those tests that the P-5 do not need at this stage. The nuclear powers continue to inflate their inventories of nuclear weapons. Therefore to safeguard our security, we refused to endorse the CTBT as it was then formulated. I foresee that even those who are making loud noises in its favour will soon depart from it.

India is always ready to go more than half way to build peace and universal disarmament, but some aspects that affect our sovereignty are non-negotiable. These, I repeat, are not negotiable. In this context, I may say that Kashmir is a part of the Indian sovereignty and our nationhood. Therefore, the question of any transaction on these matters is firmly ruled out.

With Iran and the Central Asian countries, our relationship is extremely important. We also attach a great deal of importance to our relations with China. I have already dwelt at some length on our relations with Russia, that we are keen to preserve. With the USA, our relations are improving speedily.

May I sum up by saying that India never shied away from the world. This is a part of our legacy where we view the entire world as one family (*Vasudaiva Kutumbakam*). We are vigorously adding new vistas to ensure that our diplomacy serves the nation's interests.

3

Indo-US Relations:
Start of a New Friendship*

India and the US are the world's largest and oldest democracies; thus we share certain basic beliefs, as in the rule of law and in the essential, inviolate and equal dignity of all human beings. An active engagement between us can only serve the interests of peace, stability and maintenance of humankind's democratic rights and freedoms in an increasingly uncertain world.

Chemical Weapons

India began its campaign for a nuclear weapon-free world almost as soon as it was born. Our disarmament credentials need no clarifications. We have been at the forefront of discussions leading to the Chemical Weapons Convention (CWC) because we regard this as a genuinely non-discriminatory multilateral disarmament treaty. India was among the first countries in the world to support the treaty. We actively participated in the decade-long negotiations and became an Original State Party. India was elected unopposed as the first Chairman of the

---

*Speech delivered at the meeting of Council of Foreign Relations, New York, 23/9/1997.

Executive Council of the Organization for Prohibition of Chemical Weapons (OPCW).

Nuclear Disarmament

The initiative for banning nuclear weapon tests comprehensively is a four decade-old Indian initiative. However, we refrained from signing the CTBT as it emerged in 1996. Likewise, we refused to sign the NPT as it made an arbitrary and discriminatory distinction amongst nations. Moreover, these treaties do not address our security concerns in creating a movement towards a nuclear weapon-free world but tend instead, to perpetuate a discriminatory nuclear order. With the end of the Cold War, the role and utility of nuclear weapons was reconsidered even in the United States. Many distinguished Americans have highlighted the diminishing utility of nuclear weapons and the need to do away with them in order to prevent future proliferation and enhance global security. This welcome development could provide our two countries with an opportunity to work together in an area where understanding has so far eluded us.

However, being surrounded by nuclear weapons, India cannot remain indifferent to the threat posed to its security. We did not wish to be a nuclear power, but, in the circumstances, the need to retain our nuclear option remains unavoidable.

Green Revolution

There are other areas in Indo-US relations that require reinvigoration. We were looking at cooperation in the frontier areas of science and technology. Our Green Revolution benefited greatly from US assistance as well as cooperation from American scientists. Then, as we were on the threshold of a quantum leap in our economic sphere, we remember that period with nostalgia. Some of our mechanisms for cooperation in science and

31

technology and education and culture necessitated revitalization. The need of the hour is to jointly look for innovative ways to facilitate these contacts. Our bilateral cooperation in combating narcotic trafficking and terrorism is another area in which useful and effective work had already been done and continues to be strengthened. In economic matters, any sphere of friction needs to be juxtaposed with an appreciation of long-term benefits and the perception of enduring priorities.

UN Reforms

Another area on our broader canvas must necessarily be our interest in joining other nations in the task of reforming the UN. This is an issue on which we have had some degree of dialogue. India's claim to a permanent Security Council seat is based on the strength and the global reach of its foreign policy, its commitment to the UN processes, including peace-keeping operations and on the strength of its conviction in the democratic functioning of multilateral arrangements. We believe that we qualify on the basis of any global objective and non-discriminatory criteria. We look forward to working closely with the US on the critical aspect of UN reform, as we have in the past on various other facets of UN functioning.

We are concerned with other aspects of UN reform as well. We do not see such reforms merely as an exercise to trim the budget of the world body. Instead, we feel that reforms should contribute towards a strengthened UN and its capacity to respond effectively to the priorities identified by the overwhelming majority of its membership. The concept of security should not be narrowly viewed. A world in which underdevelopment, poverty and social alienation persist can never be at peace with itself. It has been said, very truly, that 'poverty anywhere is a threat to prosperity everywhere.' Preserving international peace and stability, likewise, will require an environment where all countries are allowed a certain minimum of economic opportunity and well-being. We believe that it is in the interest of all nations to ensure that the pivotal role of the UN, as the truly global forum for the promotion of peace, security and development should be suitably reinforced.

To sum up, I believe that Indo-US relations could enter a qualitatively new phase on an objective basis in the years to come. This revitalized, reinvigorated and strengthened relationship will be moulded, in my opinion, by three distinctive realities:

Shared principles

First: our commonalities are—democracy, an open society, rule of law, pluralism and respecting the dignity of the individual. These, I believe, could become a dynamic factor in strengthening our relations. It has been said that England and the US are two countries separated by a common language. Sometimes, it appears that the US and India are two countries separated by a common political system! The time has come for us to look beyond what Sigmund Freud has called 'the narcissism of minor differences' and build on those factors which so uniquely constitute both our heritage and our commitment.

Infinite possibilities

Second: a nation of a billion people is today firmly on the path of economic reform and progress. We are committed to the goal of bringing India into the forefront of the global economy. This endeavour opens up infinite possibilities for adding new dimensions to Indo-US relations. The opportunity should not be lost.

Re-evaluation of the scope

Third: the role of India as a factor of peace and stability, in its

33

own region and beyond, must find due recognition in forging a re-evaluation of the scope and direction of Indo-US relations, in the interests of both countries.

I believe that these factors, taken together, can give a new content and thrust to the friendship between our two nations.

It is a good augury that our countries will have significant opportunities for continuing dialogue at the highest levels in the near future. I had the pleasure of meeting Senator Hillary Clinton when she was in India to attend the funeral of one of the greatest humanitarians of this century, Mother Teresa. For us in India, Mother, as she was known to millions of Indians, was a symbol of compassion. Her persona transcended mere religious definitions. Indians, whatever their religion, saw her as a lady of mercy, a living incarnation of divinity and a beacon of love, hope and care. India and the world have been orphaned by her death and Senator Clinton's presence in the moment of our grief was a gesture that we will always remember.

What has been touched upon here, represents huge challenges, beyond the capacity of any country to face on its own. This is why it is so vital for the United Nations, now more than ever before, to be a forum where we can pool creative ideas and lessons from our experience, to assist us in understanding and coping with these challenges. This is the ultimate rationale of reform. India will be ready to work with other countries to re-build the United Nations in the image of its collective aspirations and as its trusted instrument for meeting the challenges of this millennium.

Addressing the 15th regular session of the General Assembly, in October 1960, India's first Prime Minister, Pandit Jawaharlal Nehru, said:

The main purpose of the United Nations is to build up a world without war, a world based on the cooperation of

34

nations and peoples. It is not merely a world where war is kept in check for a balancing of armed forces. It is much deeper than that. It is a world from which the major causes of war have been removed and social structures built up which further peaceful cooperation within a nation as well as between nations.

It is in this spirit that we should approach the tasks before us.

4

Heritage and Promise:
India of Tomorrow*

In describing Maulana Abul Kalam Azad, Pandit Nehru had selectively chosen the word 'luminous'. Indeed, the Maulana stands out as one of the greatest luminaries not only in our struggle to win freedom, but also in shaping the contours of modern India. Panditji had once said that the Maulana combined in himself the greatness of the past, with the greatness of the present. Maulana Abul Azad was quintessentially a man representing both, through his statements and deeds, the finest traditions of Indian heritage.

Our philosopher and Statesman, Dr Sarvapalli Radhakrishnan said about the Maulana that he 'stood for what may be called the emancipation of the mind free from superstitions, obscurantism and fanaticism... Free from narrow prejudices of race or language, province or dialect, religion or caste, he worked for the ideals of national unity, probity in administration and economic progress.'

The Maulana was, as Nehru said in Parliament on his passing away, 'a curious combination of the old and the new.' Symbolizing, as he did, a glorious synthesis of cultures, civilizations,

*The Maulana Abul Kalam Azad Memorial Lecture delivered on 10/1/1998.

thoughts and philosophies, which have powerfully influenced Indian history, he was also, curiously, a bridge between the old and the new. He himself admitted that the division between the old and the new learning meant nothing to him. The old he received as his heritage, and found in his own way to confront the new, so that the paths of the new became as familiar as those of the old. Yet, Panditji, the most modern mind of our era, clearly recognized that there was in him an understanding of the 'urges of today and a modern outlook', which made him the man that he was. In fact, an editorial commented after his death: 'Azad brought to Indian nationalism the spirit of a new Renaissance, a new Reformation and a new political wisdom'.

If we think of our heritage, the first thing that will strike any objective observer is that India is distinguished by a unique civilizational continuity, which is hardly paralleled by any country in the world. For 5,000 years, Indian culture and civilization has evolved in an unbroken continuum. Of course, there have been periods of stagnation and setbacks, when the original inspiration has momentarily been overtaken by inertia, and the spark of creativity has been doused sometimes by mechanical ritualism. But, equally, there have been periods of great cultural flowerings when hardly any area of artistic endeavour has been left untouched by excellence.

Another significant element defining our heritage is that India has always represented creative assimilation rather than intolerant rejection. Many outsiders have come to India, some returned and some remained. Over the centuries those that remained became yet another strand in the infinitely complex but definitely Indian way of life. There is something about the Indian soil which allows it to retain, and over time to assimilate, the best of influences—be that of a friend or a foe.

Yet another element is the spirit of philosophical inquiry, the search for answers, the quest for knowledge, that has made our country the cradle of major religions and a home to almost all

37

the religions of the world. Many centuries before Christ, our sages, who wrote the Vedas and the Upanishads, rose above the material and the mundane to glimpse the greater reality. The great Gautama Buddha found enlightenment meditating at Bodh Gaya. Likewise, Jainism, Sikhism, Christianity and Islam have found in India not only a place to survive but an environment to flourish.

A fundamental aspect of our heritage is that the Indian society is not monolithic. On the contrary, it is, one of the most diverse societies in the world. We are a multi-ethnic, multi-religious and multilingual nation. Our geography combines deserts and seas and rivers and mountain chains which are among the longest and the tallest in the world. Our climate varies from the coldest to the hottest. Our sartorial variations would take researchers years to compile. Our social structures are such that the very rich and the very poor, the powerful and the weak, all coexist.

In 1947, through the struggle for freedom, India began the process of transition, from an enduring civilizational concept to that of a modern nation. This transition represented one of the most amazing experiments of this century. The challenge before Mahatma Gandhi, Jawaharlal Nehru, Sardar Patel, Maulana Abul Kalam Azad, and the other stalwarts of the freedom struggle was how to convert the heritage of a civilization into the promise of a nation. Much has been written about how this was achieved. But, once again, I will attempt to touch upon four key approaches, which, in my opinion, allowed this amazing drama to unfold before our very eyes. The first, I believe, was a steadfast belief in the principle of a democratic India. Our founding fathers realized that only a democracy, where every individual has the fullest freedom to express his or her political point of view, could succeed in holding together a nation where so many points of view existed. Thus, the making of democratic India was not only the result of an ideological preference, but a pragmatic understanding of ground realities.

The second factor was the conscious resolve to maintain the religious neutrality of the State. Again, the foresight and logic sustaining this approach is absolutely transparent. In a nation of such religious diversities, and, a long tradition of religious toler-ance, coexistence and harmony, the State could not but be above religious preferences, while guaranteeing, simultaneously, the fullest freedom of faith and worship to all religions.

The third factor was the pronounced tendency of the State to act in an interventionist manner to rectify the inequities in soci-ety—be they social or economic. Once again, if we reflect a little, we realize how absolutely essential such an approach was in order to foster a sense of nationhood in all Indians, to incul-cate a sense of participation in all its citizens, to the goals and values of this process of transition.

Lastly, I feel, a critical factor was the deliberate choice of retaining, in full measure, the country's independence of thought and action in its foreign policy interactions. It may not appear so obvious, but, I believe, this too fulfilled a crucial psychological need. If, subsequent to the attainment of Independence, it was perceived that the very freedom that was earned through such a profoundly ethical and uncompromising struggle, could be bar-tered away on the altar of expediency in the arena of interna-tional relations, it would devalue the struggle and render the compromise unacceptable. It was essential for all Indians to be-lieve that they were part of a process which was in conformity with the dignity of their civilisational heritage, and that the val-ues of the struggle for freedom would be preserved and ap-plied, uniformly, without differences between the internal and the external.

I believe it was with such basic tools—reflecting both ap-proach and commitment—that the promise of Indian nation-hood was launched. For all Indians, it is a reason to rejoice, as also cause to reflect. What have we achieved in these last five decades? What are our strengths? How can we nurture these strengths? What are our weaknesses, and why have some new ones assumed such an alarming profile? What yardstick do we use to judge our achievements and our failures? What goals should we set for the future?

These are but some of the questions which, on the basis of our past, and the potential of our present, must and will influence the form and content of India tomorrow. There can be little doubt that there are some very valid reasons to rejoice. In 1947 there were, I clearly recall, many distinguished observers who felt that India would not survive. For many, India was not even a nation. It was merely, as Churchill once said, 'An artificial construct, as much a nation as is the equator'. There were others who felt that once the 'paternalistic' control of the colonial power receded, India would explode into a million sterile mutinies. Many believed that India would remain dysfunctional, forever diminished by the scourge of poverty and disease. Questions were asked when Jawaharlal Nehru died, about the survival of the Indian democratic system. Many thought then that democracy would never grow strong roots in a country where feudalism had reigned undisturbed for so long. There were people, in 1947, who felt that India had more to do with maharajas and snake-charmers than with the attributes of a resurgent nation.

I believe that the real promise of India lies in its abilities to have proved such Cassandras, such prophets of doom, resoundingly wrong.

For me, the survival of India is not a matter of academic inference but a glorious reality, a benediction. Perhaps my sense of faith and optimism in the destiny of my country is excessive. Maybe. But, I have not the slightest hesitation in saying that, if we were to draw a balance sheet of what our achievements are today in order to assess what our promise will be tomorrow, I believe the pros will outnumber the cons. Democracy is a way of life in the India of today. It has grown deep roots. More people vote in a general election in India than the entire population of Europe. Again, while there may be differences of approach and emphasis, I believe that all Indians are fully committed to the preservation and strengthening of our pluralism, our tradition of tolerance, and respect for all religions. Far from being a matter of debate, the unity of India is no longer even a question. All Indians are committed to India because, in the last five and a half decades, they have had ample reason to understand, that it is only in doing so that they can best promote their own interests.

I do concede that the grand symphony that animates a democratic society is sometimes less clearly heard in the medley of voices that echo, rebound and reverberate in the spontaneous interactions of an open society. There is, indeed, occasionally the discordant voice as well. But we must realize that this new assertiveness, even aggression, is often a symptom of people becoming more aware of their democratic rights. This is the natural process in the evolution of a democracy. It is this greater assertiveness—of people and classes hitherto more compliant, and of regions hitherto less represented—which is, in a real sense, the greatest tribute to Indian democracy.

In the economic sphere too, we have done well, but we could have definitely done better. Many countries have been unable to resist the temptation, of achieving certain economic goals at the cost of effectively curtailing the right to dissent and the freedom of expression. But in India, the democratic spirit been instrumental in creating change. And, the truth is that a great deal has indeed been achieved in the last fifty years, peacefully and within a democratic framework. The Green Revolution has made us self-sufficient as far as our food requirements go, with even a degree of surplus for export. We have a diversified industrial base. Our reservoir of skilled as also untrained manpower is one of the most extensive in the world. In many areas

41

of scientific research, we are at the cutting edge. Our entrepreneurs possess talent and drive. The economic reform process enjoys support across the political spectrum. The vital indicators are positive. Our foreign exchange reserves have risen steadily and our economic growth has been good. A new middle class has emerged, which according to some estimates, is as much as the entire population of India at the time of its independence.

There is, therefore, reason to rejoice, to look back with some degree of satisfaction, at what has been achieved. But if we are to talk of the India of tomorrow, there can be no room for complacency. The battle has just begun, and is far from being fully won. The pledge has been made, but not yet fully redeemed. The dream has been seen, but has yet to become, in full measure, a reality.

If we want to make the India of tomorrow live up to its promise, and the potential inherent in our collective heritage, what must we do? We have successfully crossed two landmarks: the Golden Jubilee of our freedom and the threshold of the new millennium. This is the time for clarity, for vision, for an ability to rise above narrow considerations, and work for the good of India as a whole. It is the moment to understand that a nation grows as much through a process of reflection as by deeds. It is the occasion to comprehend that a people come into their own as much by restraint as by resolve. It is the juncture to realize that a country matures not only through a blind acceptance of the given, but equally through the exercise of the right choices.

What are the choices which India must exercise in the future? I am absolutely clear that the first imperative is the empowerment of that India which is still battling with the problems of hunger, shelter and disease. Indians, who are somewhat better off, need to free themselves once and for all of the illusion that the nation can move forward without a large section of its population. There cannot be two Indias in one: one living at the edge of change and the other immobile; one living at the edge of globalization and the other resigned to marginalization. The need to temper growth with equity was a legacy of the founding fathers of our nation. The time has come for a proper implementation of that legacy. The imperative of today is to move beyond intention to actual change at the groundlevel. The challenge today is not so much the mere articulation of goals, but the ability of these goals to transform real lives. India cannot be great if nearly half its population is illiterate; India can never tap its full potential if its women are not given their due; and India cannot truly fulfil its potential if so many of its people still suffer and die from malnutrition.

A second precondition to forge the new India of tomorrow is the strengthening of the forces of federalism within our polity. India is too vast and too diverse to be ruled by the uniformity of an excessively centralized State. It must allow the fullest representation of its great diversities and this can only be possible within the framework of a vibrant and cooperative federalism. I believe that a polity which progressively makes this possible will strengthen the unity of the nation. I have personal experience of presiding over a Cabinet which has representation from almost every part of the country and which enables all the regions of the country to have the chance of direct participation in national governance. This is especially important because the India of tomorrow will be the India of new opportunities. Its people will find novel ways and awareness of expressing themselves. They will be exposed to new influences. They will be prodded and prompted by new aspirations. This will be an India teeming with desire and expectation. For such an India to be cohesive, it must be truly representative. And representativeness in India can only be fully ensured by strengthening the unity of the country through the forces of a decentralized federalism at all levels—from village Panchayats upwards.

Also imperative is to take a very serious look at some of the aberrations which have crept into the functioning of our democracy. The fact that India is the world's largest democracy is not in dispute. What is in dispute is often the calibre and the quality that infuses the democratic canvas. The loss of ethics, of values, of principles, of a sense of rectitude, of balance, of probity and of basic honesty, is there for all to see. For a democracy to be truly great, people must not only have the freedom of choice—not between the bad and the worse, but between the best and the better. It is a matter of deep regret that criminals have found refuge in the political process. Some of those who should have been in jail, are today in state legislatures and even in Parliament. Such a situation makes a mockery of the very freedoms which democracy is meant to nurture. I have often said that the ballot box is an icon in the temple of democracy. There is a prime need to restore decency and basic virtues in public life. Unless this happens, people will lose faith in the efficacy of the democratic system. This would be an unmitigated tragedy.

Another aspect, demanding clear-headed choices, relates to our foreign policy interactions. India will benefit by emerging as a factor of peace and stability in its region. This does not for a moment imply that we become in any way less sensitive to our national interests. What this does imply, however, is a larger vision, an ability to see beyond the immediate, with a view to pursue our long-term interests. A significant step in this direction would be for us to further strengthen forums for regional cooperation, first of all, in South Asia, and also beyond, in the Indian Ocean Rim, and in Asia as a whole. We will also have to learn to use our economic strengths as a means of obtaining, through international intercourse, concrete benefits for our people. The need to preserve our independence of thought, particularly in such vital areas as security and nuclear disarmament, hardly needs to be reiterated. And finally, India will, in the years ahead, need to assert its legitimate claim to have a place in crucial decision-making bodies in major international forums, including, of course, the United Nations and the Security Council.

An India committed to working for the deprived and the downtrodden; an India committed to giving a new interpretation to the well-established maxim of Unity In Diversity; an India committed to cleansing its political process of the aberrations that have crept into it; and an India clear-sightedly pursuing its foreign policy interests. Such an India, I hope, will be the India of tomorrow—self-confident, united, democratic and strong.

I have reason to believe that there is a real basis to my hopes. Some trends are encouraging. The nation, benefiting from 50 years of nationhood, is developing some very critical consensus. Differences are indeed articulated with great vigour; but somewhere there is also the right degree of yielding, of pulling back, of understanding that in matters critical for the nation, divisions are important but unity and consensus in our national outlook is imperative too. We are also gradually developing our own self-correcting mechanisms. Of course, democracy is the greatest of them. History is about learning from mistakes. Experience comes by observing the past. Today, I see the country displaying the first signs of an ability to take corrective steps in the interests of the nation, when necessary, and by all concerned. Another great strength is the strength of institutions. A nation may be built on the foundations of good intentions, but it survives on the strength of well-established institutions. We can be proud of our ever-alert media, our vigilant judiciary and other independent bodies which give real credibility to a democracy. I am also enthused by the gradual—and some would say far too gradual—development of a coalition culture. The true test of a democracy lies in its ability to adjust to the real mandate of the people. There was a time when single party governments were possible. I believe that time is over. Coalitions will be the norm in the foreseeable future. The India of tomorrow must learn to deal with them.

I am confident that the next century will be the century of India. This is not a matter of faith alone. I genuinely believe that the best is yet to be. Our founding fathers, among whom the Maulana shone so luminously, began a journey. The journey is not yet complete. We have crossed many milestones. But the destination is still ahead, and not too distant, when the India of tomorrow will truly come into its own, fulfilling, the hopes and dreams of those who won freedom for us.

And yet, the price of this will have to be eternal vigilance—vigilance and the ability to dream, to think big, to think ahead, to rise above the small and the petty and to think, above all, of India. If we, as a nation can do this, the India of tomorrow will surpass all our expectations. But, if we don't, I can only repeat the immortal warning of Iqbal:

Agar ab bhee na samjhogey to
mit jao'gey duni'ya sey,
Tumharee dastan tak bhee
na hogee dastanon meyn.

If even now you understand not,
razed from the world you would be,
Even your story will not be found
in the annals of history.

But I am certain this is not to be, and we shall continue to be a great nation.

46

5

A Vision of the Twentieth Century*

India has always possessed a very healthy tradition of vigorous and informed debate on international issues outside the framework of the government. Think tanks and policy research institutes conducting independent surveys of developments and a government's response to them, make an important contribution to shaping national opinion on issues of international significance. A look at the prodigious work done by such bodies in other countries, and the impact it has, should make us realize its importance. The entry of the Indian Association for International Affairs (IAIA) amongst think tanks has been a welcome development, and I look forward to the contributions that it may make in shaping foreign policy issues.

As we step into the twenty-first century, there is an air of expectation. The new century may present some new challenges, it may perhaps make some fundamental changes in the affairs of humankind. Yet, such expectations for change are not new. In fact, the only permanent feature of human affairs, in the previous century and throughout history, has been change itself. Societies have always had to prepare for it and cope with the unpredictable consequences of the changes. This is true today

---

*Speech delivered on the occasion of the inauguration of the Indian Association for International Affairs, New Delhi on 15/1/1997.

47

also, with the difference that change now is more rapid and gives nations and societies less time to prepare and to react to them. It is all the more important today, not only to understand what kind of change is occurring, but also how we can prepare ourselves in advance to take advantage of what it may hold in store for us.

In a historical perspective, Indian society has been in the throes of profound transformation since the beginning of the twentieth century. The freedom movement and the liberation of India fundamentally transformed the world by unleashing anti-colonial forces everywhere and setting an example of a peaceful struggle for political and social rights. Our advocacy for change, providing a lesson for peaceful transformation and conflict resolution, is appreciated the world over. India's Independence in 1947 meant that colonialism everywhere in the world was doomed. Ever since then, India has been an active agent of change in the world, providing meaning to values of participatory democracy, respect for individual faith and freedom, and a deep commitment to preserve the variety and richness in society. These are the guiding principles of a sane and humanistic world order as a whole. What we have achieved as a poor and developing society, with the inherited weight of poverty and colonial deprivation, enhances the uniqueness of India.

The transformation that India has witnessed in the past has been an important ingredient in the changing world. India accounts for nearly one-fifth of all humanity and what we have achieved or are capable of achieving, influences the potential for change everywhere. The political, social, economic and technological renewal which India has undergone in the preceeding century is a stupendous achievement by any yardstick. Future historians will no doubt record the renaissance and renewal of India, for all its obstacles, frustrations and wasted opportunities, as one of the defining features of the twentieth century. At the same time, India's adherence to certain core principles and basic tenets, while undergoing this transformation, is as much of a feature of our achievement. Gandhiji had expressed the thought that independent India must keep its windows open to the outside world and let fresh breeze come in from all directions, without allowing itself to be blown off its feet. Our basic approach to international relations also derives from this: to treat the world on equal terms without fear or favour of any sort. Just as our young Republic was guided by the principles of egalitarianism, individual liberty, respect for the equal dignity of all citizens and belief in the rule of law, so too have we sought an international order based on these principles.

Our freedom struggle was one of the defining features of the century behind us. It gave us a world view and a self image. In it were distilled the views of not only some of the greatest sons and daughters of India, but also of some of the greatest minds that the world has seen. Gandhi, Nehru, Patel, Swami Vivekananda, Rabindranath Tagore, Maulana Azad, Sarojini Naidu, Gokhale, Tilak and countless others, while talking about independence, also defined what India was and should be. The soul of India, as it were, was being regenerated even as we strove to regain Independence. It was only natural that our earliest leaders would apply themselves to the continuation of the values that drove us to independence. We did not allow those values to be negated even by an oppressive and largely colonial world order.

We consciously decided not to follow an artificial policy in our dealings with the rest of the world. The wellspring of our policy has to be those values which we ourselves have followed on our road to freedom. It was unthinkable that others would define our policies for us, or prescribe to us a model to follow. We do not intend to abdicate our rights and responsibilities to let our policies be decided by a cabal of developed nations, and that too when the premise of our newly-found freedom was to gain those very rights and responsibilities.

49

To be sure, our independent stand did not win us friends amongst the entrenched powers, but we had no illusions about our stand then, just as we have no illusions about the stand we take today on various issues of international relations. We were not out to win a popularity contest or gather certificates for good behaviour. We were out to get for others the same rights that we had fought for, rights that we believed were inalienable in any civilized society. 1947 is a seminal date not only in Indian or Asian history, but in world history. The folding up of the greatest colonial empire in history signalled to the colonial and neo-colonial powers elsewhere that these systems devised by them were about to be consigned to the dustbin of history. Our voice, howsoever lone it might have been in the beginning, had to be raised if we were to be true to ourselves. The Non-Aligned Movement was the institutionalization of this mindset.

Our belief in the Non-Aligned Movement, implying independence of thought and autonomy of action, has been and will remain an important element of our foreign policy. We do not believe that its relevance has diminished as a result of the termination of the Cold War. The Non-Aligned Movement was not a by-product of the Cold War—it was an idea developed in response to counter the inequality and the severity of entrenched imbalance in thedistribution of economic and political power and influence in the world. It was also a response of colonized people to centuries long indignity and disempowerment which their societies had suffered and the consequences of which are still with us. The NAM gave voice to those who had been silent for centuries. This point should never be lost sight of. Developing countries have no realistic option other than to frequently consult and develop common positions and approaches which safeguard their rights and national interests, if they are to maintain their independence and dignity. India, for its part, would continue to play a constructive role in bringing the developing countries together and jointly articulating their viewpoint.

50

More relevant is how the Non-Aligned Movement should re-engineer itself to face the challenges of a changing world. Independence of thought and autonomy of choice will continue to be the hallmarks of the Movement, and it would be a pity if it continued to be misunderstood as it was in the beginning. The Movement needs to look at new areas of cooperation amongst its members. The commercial, economic and technological areas immediately come to mind and some worthwhile work has already been done in these areas. The potential that exists, however, is vast. We must pool our energies and resources to find answers to our common problems. It would also be desirable for us to consult each other on issues of international concern and develop common positions in order to further protect our interests.

India gave the world the concept of the world as a single family. Peace amongst nations and the security of the whole world has been the other basic tenet of our foreign policy. Our concern and our commitment were reflected even before Independence, we were among the founder members of the United Nations. Our belief was that such a body was required to help maintain peace and minimize disorder wherever it occurred. Barely half a dozen years into our own Independence, we were asked to serve on UN commissions looking after two of the most serious issues that erupted in the immediate post-World War II years—the Israeli-Palestinian conflict and the Korean War.

As I have stated before, the UN needs to be strengthened and its continued credibility requires the reform of the organization. While the membership of the UN has increased greatly, the voices of the newly sovereign states remain unheard. There is an imbalance in the authority and weight of various structures or organs. The Security Council needs to be made more representative in order to enhance its effectiveness. The vast increase in the membership of the UN since its founding, especially of the developing countries, must find adequate representation in the

51

permanent as well as non-permanent categories. Reform and expansion must be an integral part of a common package, addressing not only the failings of the past, but also the needs of the future.

We believed, as now, at the time of our Independence, that equitable development for the nations of the world was impossible without a peaceful world where the security of all nations was ensured. The totally irrational arms race that characterized the worst Cold War years, not only prevented development, as funds were diverted from developmental areas to armaments, but also enhanced global insecurity, as the rest of the world lived in the constant shadow of a looming nuclear holocaust.

India took the lead seeking global nuclear disarmament and was amongst the first countries responsible for inscribing it on the UN agenda in the mid-fifties. Our viewpoint was that nuclear weapons were inherently destabilizing and that the sooner the planet was rid of the last nuclear weapon, the better it would be for the security of the whole world. The view was ignored. On the other hand, half-baked, discriminatory and ad hoc measures such as the NPT and the CTBT formed the core of the response of the status quo powers. What happened with the CTBT was particularly disappointing because we felt that the international community had let slip an opportunity to bring about true disarmament. The fact that the treaty violates international laws in imposing obligations on a sovereign state that has clearly expressed its opposition to the treaty is probably one of its lesser failures.

The cost of the nuclear arms race has been gruesome, to use a term associated with war. Some estimates put it at nearly one trillion dollars. What could have been possible with those funds is anybody's guess. As for India, our position is clear. We will never sign treaties that do not accept global nuclear disarmament as the primary objective. Contrary to perception, we were not the only ones who held such views, in spite of the vote in the

UN where other factors come into play. Our position was endorsed by the NAM Heads of State at their Summit in Columbia. The International Court of Justice recognized the pursuit and conclusion of negotiations on nuclear disarmament as an obligation for all states. All over the world, major non-governmental organizations and former armed forces personnel were calling for the elimination of nuclear weapons. Until there was credible movement in this direction, any constraints on ourselves were unacceptable.

The concept that the world is one family comes from the realization that the earth is indivisible. Whatever happens to some of us will, one day, happen to all of us. We face the daunting challenges of international terrorism, large-scale environmental degradation, inter-ethnic rivalry and revivalist nationalism, all of which are transactional phenomena and none of which will stop at or respect national borders. An international concert is required to tackle these and the associated problems of under-development for large populations of the world.

From the beginning, India's policy has been to pursue friendship and cooperation with everybody, especially its neighbours. In the South Asian region, we have made consistent attempts trying to implement policies that build confidence and enhance cooperation amongst ourselves. I enunciated a five-point policy which takes as its basis non-interference in the affairs of our neighbours, and respect for their sovereignty. The 'Gujral Doctrine', states that first, with neighbours like Bangladesh, Bhutan, Maldives, Nepal and Sri Lanka, we do not ask for reciprocity but give what we can in good faith. Second, no South Asian country should allow its territory to be used against other countries of the region. Third, no one country will interfere in the internal affairs of another. Fourth, all South Asian countries must respect each other's territorial integrity and sovereignty. And finally, everyone will settle all their disputes through peaceful bilateral negotiations. If implemented sincerely, these principles are sure

to recast South Asia's relationships in a more friendly and cooperative mould. The implementation of these principles would
generate a climate of close and mutually benign cooperation in
our region, where the weight and size of India is regarded positively and as an asset by these countries, and we have succeeded to a large measure in generating this confidence. We
have achieved considerable mileage with this approach. As I
have stated before, our policy led to significant breakthrough in
our relationships with Bangladesh and Nepal.

A feature of the economic transformation of many regions of
the world has been a qualitative enhancement of regional cohesion and cooperation. There has been a virtual proliferation of
groupings as nations seek to maximize the potential benefits of
removing artificial barriers between themselves. In the industrialized world, not only economic but, to some extent, even national identities have become blurred within this larger purpose.
In some parts of the developing world, this process is under way
and has already led to some spectacular results in a few regions.

The South Asian region cannot remain immune from this
logic of collective self-interest. Both, through our Chairmanship
of SAARC, as well as in dealings with our neighbours, we have
tried to advance, with some success, a spirit of shared self-interest. As I stated before the historic decision to strive for a South
Asian Free Trade Area (SAFTA) latest by the year 2005, was
taken, after the launching of the South Asian Preferential Trade
Arrangement (SAPTA). Many new areas of cooperation in the
economic and cultural fields have been identified. Ministerial
level interaction was picking up. Our chairmanship was gaining
recognition from member-states as dynamic and forward looking. We sought to advance cohesion, synergy and mutual goodwill in our region so that it would fully participate in a resurgent
Asia and indeed the world.

With China, we sought relations of stability and mutual benefit, realizing the potential for favourable growth where it exists

54

and not allowing areas of differences to cast a shadow on the entire relationship, while addressing them squarely. This was the tenor during the visit of the Chinese President.

The Central Asian region lies in one of the external circles which form a part of our proximate neighbourhood. We established missions in all Central Asian states and reached a high level of productive dialogue with them. We were also deeply concerned about the developments in Afghanistan and had clearly stated that they ran counter to the principles we espouse. We succeeded in having our traditional role of a friend and well-wisher of Afghanistan recognized through the invitations extended to us to participate in the conferences on Afghanistan in Teheran and the United Nations.

In the wider world, our interaction with major political and economic centres, be it the USA, Russia, the European Union and its members, or Japan, has been a constructive and amicable one, with the advancement of economic ties being a principal feature. With Russia, our relations have been characterized by continuity, trust and mutual understanding. Transitional difficulties, which impinged on our ties with Russia at the start of the Cold War era, are well behind us. Both countries recognized the strategic dimensions of the relations which were developing in a dynamic and multi-faceted manner.

We continued to remain committed to our relationship with the countries of Africa and Latin America. One of the most significant initiatives in this aspect has been the G-15, of which India continues to be an active member. Through this forum, we hope to achieve the twin objectives of South-South cooperation and North-South dialogue, by bringing together the developmental experiences of nations from three vast continents.

Let me also point out here that where our world-views were not compatible with those of others, or where we had to make clear our national interests against the pressure of conformity, we did it with firmness, clarity and maturity, for which we were

55

duly recognized. We were willing to cooperate with everyone but refuse to tag ourselves in advance to a particular world-view or to a group of countries. We examined each issue on its merits, being guided at all times by our vital interests and concerns.

The attempt to conceive a better ordering of human society than the cruel and destructive chaos in which it has hitherto existed is by no means modern. Whether the predicament of human society is better then than, say a century ago, is a moot point. What is more important is that the modern world, with the spread of education and developments in technology and communications, has produced new conditions, more favourable than ever before, for a radical reconstruction. However, the will and the design for bringing about seminal change still seems to be incomplete. There are too many armaments around. There is too much suspicion, and too little trust. The politics of power, whether open or concealed, of domination and of reluctance to create space for emerging players, continue to characterize international relations. The Cold War may be over for some of us, but the adversarial vocabulary and mindset in foreign relations has not really diminished.

In this scenario, India's role, along with others, should be to create a democratic world order in spirit and fact. We must aim for a world free of animosity and hatred, unfettered by deprivation of any kind, and devoted to the perpetual quest for human happiness. This is what we owe to our children and succeeding generations.

The policy and the vision of India, as we moved into the twenty-first century, were well-defined. We did not spell them out in terms of tactical or strategic doctrines. We sought to project them in the ambience of our cultural ethos and historical experiences. India has derived a message from the unique character of its freedom struggle, which is simple but revolutionary in its precepts and practices. The world and its people need peace, security, development and a just society. Therefore, the Indian quest in the coming years must help and assist in trying to make this dream a reality.

The foreign policy of India must remain an effective instrument to meet this 'tryst with destiny'. This could be achieved by forging and sustaining a national consensus around these principles.

57

6

Some Thoughts on the Soviet Collapse*

The dramatic changes in the Soviet Union are not easy to comprehend. What we witnessed was a dissembling of history, of much that has gone to make and un-make in this century.

We saw the discarding of communism by the leaders and people of the Soviet Union and the banning of the Communist Party of the Soviet Union (CPSU). The dissolution of the great Soviet State left the world benumbed since no one could ever foresee this.

A century and a half ago, Marx and Engels wrote the *Communist Manifesto* and launched communism. Marx expected the first communist revolution to occur in one of the three countries that he regarded were 'civilised'—Germany, Britain and France. History, however, proved him wrong. The first communist revolution took place in a semi-feudal Russia which was an empire built on the foundations of colonialism.

It was Lenin, not Marx, who then applied the Marxian doctrines to establish the first Socialist State. Lenin died within a decade of the Bolshevik Revolution, leaving it to Josef Stalin to build the mighty dictatorship; with whiplash industrialisation and forced collectivization of agriculture; and a massive helping of terror as an instrument of Socialist construction. The result was

---

*Dr Parulekar Memorial Lecture, delivered at Pune on 30/9/1990.

the creation of industrial power in a span of 20 years, a power that could take on and crush the mighty armies of Adolf Hitler to the tremendous amazement of the entire world. The accomplishments of the USSR made many men and women all over the world turn their eyes away from its shortcomings and terrible aberrations. While on the contrary some sensitive individuals turned away crying that the gods of revolution had failed them. For most of the outside observers like us, wrote novelist Graham Greene, 'Communists have committed great crimes, but at least they have not stood aside, like an established society, and indifferent. I would rather have blood on my hands than walk away like the Pilate.'

Jawahar Lal Nehru and Rabindranath Tagore both saw with their eyes and felt with their senses the darker sides of the Soviet experiment. But what created a much greater and more enduring impression on their great minds was the extraordinary achievements of the USSR in mass education and health, in a great flowering of the arts and music and dance, and an almost painfully oppressive longing for the future liberation of humankind from shackles of poverty, inequality and injustice.

The Soviet State dominated world politics for most of the twentieth century. The Allies of World War I intervened to dismember the infant USSR. The Allies of World War II were determined to contain it and roll back its influence from Eastern Europe. It was the mythical Fatherland of all revolutions, it had the tremendous ego to claim the direction of all revolutions anywhere on the earth.

After World War II, the USSR became the Other Superpower inspite of all its technological weaknesses and its lags in democracy and human rights. During the Cold War, the Soviet Union claimed parity with the United States and was conceded parity not only in strategic nuclear weapons but also as leader of a rival international system challenging the might and power of the capitalist system.

And then, suddenly, that mighty state lay prostrate. Its creed and doctrine, communism, was in disgrace. Not because it has been defeated in a traditional war by a mightier power, but because its leader, Mikhail Gorbachev, inspired by stirring visions of the future not only of his own homeland but also of the entire humankind, was determined to transform a seventy-year-old rugged dictatorship into a social democracy drawing its life-blood from the free consent of its deeply diverse population. This unique background to the collapse of the communist state in the USSR imparts to the tragedy a nobility that must not escape.

'In every great change', wrote Nobel laureate Anatole France, 'we leave behind us a part of ourselves, we must die to one life before we enter into another.' What we witnessed before our eyes was the dying of one way of life of 240 million people and its rebirth as another.

The causes of the collapse, however, will continue to puzzle and torment thousands of people all over the world for years to come. India is too close to the Great Dissolution to be capable of an objective, clinical judgement. All the same one could say the end of Cold War did not go in favour of the Soviets. Human history had never witnessed a Cold War earlier and had not visualized its consequences for the defeated side. We are now slowly grasping them.

The collapse certainly gladdened Cold Warriors all over the world, especially in the United States and Western Europe. Their verdict was accentuated and carried by the electronic media to the far corners of the earth, i.e. the failure of Communism and the triumph of Capitalism. The President of France, Francois Mitterand, observed that 'The revolution that gained its momentum in Moscow with Mikhail Gorbachev's perestroika, and which, having gone round the Central and Eastern European capitals under communist control, came back to Moscow for its completion and is raising questions for the whole of Europe'.

In other words, Perestroika did to the Soviet state in 1991 what it had accomplished in Central and Eastern Europe in 1989. Perestroika means restructuring, rebuilding a political society. In the rebuilding of the Central and East European states, with the bricks and mortars of the market, West European assistance was immediately available, while Gorbachev himself provided the assured framework of a stable transition. However, the change-over did affect the life of millions of people in ways they were hardly ready for, and these newly transformed market economies would require at least a decade, perhaps even longer, to find their feet in the prosperous community of West Europeans. Meanwhile, they are described as the 'Third World' of the affluent West, who have a stronger claim to the latter's generous hands of assistance than that of the real Third World.

The former Soviet Union was three times the size of India. It carried in its shattered bodipolitik 15 republics; hundreds of ethnic communities—with their languages and cultures and historical memories; and its geography extended from the Baltics in the West to Siberia in the East. The state that Stalin had built had turned into a disjointed group of many nations.

What kept the former USSR together all these three score and ten years and more? This is the most tormenting question that we must seek answers for. Was it the ideology of Communism with its egalitarian appeal, its promise to build a higher and nobler civilization? But the people of the USSR and Eastern Europe turned against communism with a fury no one expected or accounted for, including, I dare say, Mikhail Gorbachev. The 19 million members of the CPSU seemed to have accepted its collapse with instant surrender. The coup illustrated the epic disarray of the communists of the Soviet Union. It failed even before it could muster the strength to stand on its feet. Like all coups, it gravely distorted the foundations of the political society, and accelerated the pace of decay and collapse. The coup robbed Gorbachev of whatever resources and opportunities he had, to work out an orderly transition from communism to social democracy.

What is a transition? A famous political philosopher of the nineteenth century, John C. Calhoun, described transition as 'the interval between the decay of the old and the establishment and formation of the new'. 'A transition', he observed, 'must necessarily be a period of uncertainty, confusion, error and wild and fierce fanaticism'.

We find some of these aspects of transition in our own country too as we move from a single-party dominated polity to a highly pluralistic multi-party, one. The accents of chaos and confusion in the Soviet Union were far deeper and louder. This brings us back us to the question that I asked above: What made the great and mighty Soviet State collapse so rapidly into a welter of mutually warring nations or nationalities, of clashing nationalist aspirations and economic decay?

Evidently, Communism as an ideological cement could not hold the USSR together, as the command-and-control political system and the totally centralized economy was being dismantled. Suddenly, the accumulated feelings of 350 million people, bottled for 70 years by an inviolable dictatorship, gushed forth with a fury that few could anticipate. The failures and shortcomings of the Soviet experiment looked much larger than its accomplishments.

As Indian Ambassador for five years, I myself saw many of these failures—the gross inequalities between the privileged governing class of communists and the mass of ordinary people; the not altogether suppressed nationalist sentiments; the failure of the system to bring the fruits of a massive industrial revolution to the doors of its citizens in the form of material comforts. The deprivations were obvious but there were also the unquestionable achievements of Soviet science and technology. There was the large modern infrastructure which stretched from the Baltics to the Pacific waters and there was the great international role of a Superpower.

But when the breeze which carried the whiff of change turned into a whirlwind the people of the USSR cared little for the Communist achievements. They suddenly woke up to their diverse nationalist urges, to ancient olden tradition of religiosity, and showed an awesome craving for the creature comforts of advanced capitalist democracies which eclipsed from the minds the once-hallowed appeal of Communism.

Gone with the winds of change were many myths of the past. The Nationality Policy of Stalin, in the crafting of which the Indian Marxist thinker and activist MN Roy also had a hand, was held up as the solution to the nationality problems of all multinational states. It had 'solved' the national question in the USSR for all time, we were told. But reality treated us to an entirely different picture. Not only was the nationality problem in the USSR not resolved, it had in fact been brewing all the while, accumulating its corrosive grievances and senses of deprivation. And as soon as Glasnost and Perestroika lifted the shackles of dictatorship, it gushed out as a mighty flood and almost washed away the state of the proletariat that was built over a period of seven decades.

The republics were declaring their independence. In Georgia, the Ukraine, Moldavia, Armenia, Azarbaijan and even in the Central Asian republics, the desire to break away from the Russian rulers of the past seemed stronger than the wisdom to stay together in a world where integration of Sovereign States had become one of the megatrends of global change.

The conclusion is unavoidable that it was the dictatorship, the command-and-control political system, the denial of democratic rights to the people that lay at the roots of the Soviet collapse. No amount of casuistry can hide this fact from the people of the world. This hard fact must change the basic outlook of leftists, progressives and revolutionaries all over the world.

A huge debate was steadily welling up in the anguished minds of Marxists and Socialists in many countries.

I do not want to dwell on the puzzlements, dilemmas and agonies inflicted on the minds of radical leftists including myself and all over the world by the collapse of Soviet communism and the proletariat state in the USSR. However, some questions do come to my mind and will have to find convincing answers in the current debates.

Is Marxism-Leninism going to be confined only to the agrarian societies of the developing world while the industrialized and post-industrial societies of the North, returns to social democracy? Can proletariat dictatorship succeed in the present epoch of technological and information revolution? And that too in a global upsurge of the democratic urges of humankind? Will democracy in the real sense of the term, with social and economic substance as well as political liberties, and human rights, also in their widest sense, replace socialism and communism as the major guideline of the struggles of the denied, the deprived, the exploited and the oppressed all over the world? The struggle of these people for a better life and a better deal in their own societies must continue and will continue because capitalism inspite of its relatively high threshold of social protection leaves many problems of human development cynically untouched.

Perhaps the forms of struggle, its ideological language and operational thrusts will change. And perhaps with the passage of time, but before the end of the century, we will find winds of democracy blowing into a majority of the societies of the Third World too.

The new hierarchy is roughly as follows: There is a State Council presided over by the President of the Union and is made up of Presidents of the Republics and is incharge of overall coordination of foreign and domestic policies. The Supreme Soviet has two chambers—a 332-member Council of Republics that deals with republican matters and a Council of the Union.

Under the State Council, there is an Inter-Republican Committee, endowed with special responsibility for the economy of the entire Union. And, finally, there are the Republican Ministries and Union Ministries, the latter substantially reduced in number. The overall framework is federal or confederal, and there is a tremendous devolution of power and resources from the Union to the Republics. This edifice was not easy to construct.

On the contrary what was in the offing was an entirely new Europe. President Mitterand expected the birth of a new Europe of at least 33 states, if not more, which he visualized would come together as a single European Home. Whether his expectations then were too optimistic or not, the new Russian state, not committed to socialism but retaining a high threshold of social protection, could identify itself with Europe rather than with other socialist countries. It was already in the process of disengagement from Cuba, Afghanistan and Vietnam. Its friendly relations with China do not wear any ideological patina. Its huge market will allure the leading industrial powers—the Americans, the Germans and other West Europeans and the Japanese.

Perhaps in the future, competition and rivalries among the industrial powers may increase, and we may see much American effort made to keep the new Russia on its side. The very large community of Slavic Americans may pressurise for this to happen.

There is not much of surplus capital in the world, and there are countries who are eagerly seeking investment and aid and whose voice carries more weight than ours—Russia is one of the leading candidates now—and the image of India the world over is still that of a democracy beset with a minority government and an overload of internal conflicts. We must summon the will of the nation to resolve our internal conflicts, build a peaceful home front and peaceful cooperative relations with our neighbours.

We must seek new pastures of significant cooperation with countries close to us—the ASEAN bloc, South Korea, the countries of West Asia and the leading members of the Latin American community. In short, we need a grand strategy of national peace, regional cooperation and larger economic and political relations with the rest of the world.

Looking beyond the clouds of today's misfortunes to the horizons of the future, I foresaw our relations with a reborn Russian state acquiring a new vigour and newer thrusts of cooperative development. There is a great fund of goodwill and friendship for India among the Russian people, as there is a great reservoir of affection in India for Russia. India and the former USSR had mingled together in objective as well as subjective fields of understanding and friendship for thirty years, creating a very large pool of non-conflicting visions and perspectives. This great fund of human relations will need to pull together in days fair or foul.

We must continue to focus on the fate and future of Central Asian republics with whom we have had close relationships in all phases of history. The lavas of every socio-political eruption there have sooner or later, flown into our lands. The dogma based polity there—whatever its other demerits, had modernized and secularized the region's medieval societies. Any reversal of this phenomenon could bring in fundamentalisms and civil wars that could cast a long shadow on our subcontinent too.

Afghanistan has always been of vital geo-strategic interest to us. The Russians had backed out of their commitments to supply arms to the Kabul regime. It was difficult to say whether the USA would encourage the fundamentalist segments of the Mujahideens to ascend or let a moderate coalition of various factors emerge. At present the situation is very fluid and calls for a great deal of diplomatic vigilance and activity on our part.

A reborn Russia must continue to meet us as old partners of a new world order. Let me end on a note of optimism reflected in the following quotation from Rabindranath Tagore:

66

When old words die out on the tongue,
New melodies break out from the heart,
And where the old tracks are lost,
New country is revealed with its wonders.

7

Coalition Politics Come of Age

In India, as in other established democracies, the chief agents of political change are the people. People elect the government at the Centre and in the states; it is up to the people, the voters, to determine whether to renew or deny the mandate to the ruling party. In India, as in other democracies, the *voter is king*. It also happens to be India's proud privilege that the voters number over six hundred million; they speak many languages, live a diverse cultural life, but are politically united in a single nation state, a federal Union, in which the states enjoy considerable autonomy. To describe India as the largest democracy in the world is not just a cliché. When more than a billion people, caught in the excitement and anguish of change and development, in a society that is still in many respects underdeveloped, are trained in the creative art of democratic self-government, it is a political event, a political phenomenon of unprecedented dimensions and significance in the political history of humankind.

In the parliamentary election of November 1989 and the state assembly polls of February 1990, the sovereign voters of India determined, first, to demolish the predominance of a single party in India's political life, and, secondly to hand down a truly multi-party regime. The process of dismantling India's single party dominant system, started between 1967-69, but took 20 years to gain momentum.

The political map of India created by the two elections of 1989 granted power at the centre to the National Front, a coalition of the Janata Dal and a number of regional parties. It was a minority government with majority support in the Lok Sabha, provided by its two allies, the Left Front on the one hand and the Bharatiya Janata Party (BJP) on the other. The Janata Dal had power in three states—with minority governments in Uttar Pradesh and Bihar, and a majority government in Orissa. The Congress (I) governed three states, two in the South—Andhra Pradesh and Karnataka, with majority governments, and one, in Maharashtra with a minority government. BJP was in power in two states—Himachal Pradesh and Madhya Pradesh. The rest of India was governed by coalition governments without the Congress-I. They were led by a Marxist coalition in West Bengal and Kerala, Janata Dal and BJP coalitions in Rajasthan and Gujarat, and regional party regimes in Assam and Tamil Nadu. This was the political map of India in the year of global change in international as well as domestic politics. Depending on the mood, one can describe the political picture either as a rainbow or a zebra.

I would prefer to describe the scenario then as an enduring transition from a single dominant party system to a durable multiparty political system. It remains enduring because the voters in the coming years have not shown any tendancy to return to the dominant supremacy of a single party of our political life. We have perhaps pitched firmly for coalition politics, an inevitable phase in the political history of today's mature parliamentary democracies, a historical fact we often tend to forget. Almost all the parliamentary democracies of Europe have passed through coalitional systems to arrive at stable two-party systems; even now, several European countries are governed by coalitions. With India's great diversities, its different cultural and linguistic groups increasingly politicized, coalitions appear to be inevitable in our journey towards a mature and developed democratic republic. We have acquired considerable coalitional experience at the State level. At the Centre, the government of 1989 was the second experiment in a coalition of different parties. This fact alone lends it a tremendous importance in the growth of Indian polity. The vast national electorate, more than double the size of the entire population of the United States, needs to have confidence in an alternative to the largest party; it has to earn national credibility. The only alternative, given India's political system, can be a coalition of parties.

What was the significance of this political change in India for our people and for our democracy? Was it a landmark between long years of political stability followed by a long period of political instability? How can a single dominant party render unto a society of 800 million people a stable and orderly government? How can it be expected to navigate through troubled political and economic waters that governments happen to face everywhere? These and other similar questions gnawed at the minds of international and Indian observers of the Indian political scene. In an age of theatrical media reporting, with conflict and crisis the staple of the press, the dynamics of Indian politics, the inevitable clashes of perspectives and priorities of coalition partners often gets dramatized. Seasoned and spiced with free-market speculation and rumours, political news from India tended to create an impression that the world's largest democracy was teetering on the edge of chaos.

The reality was very different. Considerable innovativeness of our political leaders was illustrated by the coalition government at the Centre in India in 1989. The three main parties of the 'outer coalition'—the National Front, the Left Front and the BJP—adopted an agreed-upon programme aimed at extending and enriching democracy. It is this programme that won the voter's mandate.

The political alliance between the different parties that constituted the National Front formulated a national platform of

70

democratic extension, which included autonomy for the electronic media, substantial decentralization of power and resources from the Centre to the states, from the states to panchayats or village councils, which also included a bold agenda for expanding human rights for women, youth, the socially and economically backward classes and the minorities. The platform promised a massive rural thrust in development planning, a better deal for farmers, and a frontal and spatial attack on mass poverty. It is these promises of social justice that won the National Front the voters' mandate to govern.

The government's determination to translate the platform's promises into legislation and later, to implement the laws whipped up a climate of 'instability'. My government came to power to build a new democratic polity, to bring about a new era of social forces with a view to broadening the political reach and social content of our democracy. In ten months, streams of change flowed onto the political process and into the political economy of development.

We had passed a legislation conferring an autonomous status on the electronic mass media, i.e. radio and television. Television was watched by 72 per cent of our population; it no longer remained an instrument of propaganda in the hands of government. We set up the Centre-State Council, provided for in the Constitution but never implemented by the Congress governments. The Council was a significant step in expanding the federal fabric of the Indian Union. We made all land reform laws immune to litigation. We set up a Women's Commission with powers to improve the social and economic condition of women. We granted adequate privileges to the Minorities Commission and also to the Commission for Scheduled Castes and Tribes enabling the two bodies to enforce laws prohibiting social and cultural discrimination. We also introduced in the Parliament, legislation providing for an unprecedented decentralization of power and resources to a new Panchayat system, making peri-

71

odical elections, on the basis of political parties, mandatory, and not left to the wishes and whims of the state governments.

At the economic level, my government decided to invest 50 per cent of development resources in the rural areas and declared the 1990s to be the decade of the farmers. We increased the prices of farm produce for bulk buying by government agencies and we forgave loans given to middle and poor farmers as an incentive to greater production. We took bold measures to make the domestic economy more competitive, removing many restrictions on the establishment of medium and small industries and cutting down heavily on bureaucratic red-tape. Without weakening the national resolve to protect our economic independence, we opened the Indian economy to foreign investment and collaboration. We inherited a near-empty exchequer; we were operating in the midst of a difficult, even bleak, international economic environment made much worse for us by the Gulf crisis. But we were determined not to push India into a debt trap.

The Government's decision to implement an election pledge to reserve 27 per cent of jobs in the Central Government and State-run industries for what is known in India as Other Backward Classes (OBCs) created an emotional storm in India and led to violent protests and, unfortunately, to loss of life. We were accused of unleashing a war of castes. Nothing was further from the truth. The Prime Minister had proposed a dialogue with the protesters. In India, we have a long cultural tradition of tolerance and resolving differences through dialogue and mutual accommodation. The affirmative discrimination in favour of the backward classes or castes was aimed at bringing these lower strata of our society into the power structure. Mass poverty, the Prime Minister declared, was not an economic issue but a political issue. The poor and the deprived need to be brought into the power structure in order to make the system really work for social justice.

72

We were in the midst of transition from the single-dominant party system to a genuinely democratic multiparty system. The flavour of change was all pervasive; but the taste was not altogether sweet.

In the United States, the states have emerged in the last ten years from the twilight that had shrouded them for decades; they are now seen to be more energetic, assertive and innovative. A kindred process has begun in India. We have imparted to the great bulk of our people living in the huts and hamlets of rural India, the backward classes and castes, the poor and the exploited, the minorities, the harijans and the tribal folk, a creative stir they have not enjoyed for years. This is how a democracy laden with mass poverty but still moving from one landmark of progress to another, must evolve to a higher level of politics of participation, of power-sharing between today's haves and have-nots.

A Radical Change*

Since the changing world relations highlight new factors, diplomacy is now far more complex. The complexity keeps on increasing; only the myopic would believe that foreign policies can be formulated at the behest of foreign offices alone. It cannot be. It is important that academics, experts from various fields, and research scholars, not only from the sphere of International Affairs but also from several other spheres, make their contributions.

The people who work in the administration realize that a Minister in our system is never an expert on a specific subject; he formulates a view on the basis of the various options offered to him. He then decides on one or the other of the options presented to him. It is very important that we encourage our thinkers, experts, academics to participate in the structuring of the country's foreign policy, especially in the post-Second World era.

Diplomacy is not the exclusive preserve of the elite. Neither is it a preserve of the foreign office. Democratic space has expanded a great deal, as has education, knowledge and information about world affairs. Information technology has undergone

---

*Lecture delivered under the auspices of the Institute of Asian Studies at the Administrative Staff College of India, Hyderabad on 30/6/1990.

dramatic changes. Radical transformation of communication methodology has left a deep impact on the methods and styles of diplomacy. On what basis is a foreign policy made?

In the contemporary era, we have to pool all resources and take a view of India's stature. In the days gone by, diplomacies were confined to political relations alone. Now it must address scientific and technological cooperations, economic cooperation and, of course, assess in depth if the security perceptions vary. Therefore, it is imperative that all these factors are kept in mind and for this, experts of these subjects are invited to make their contributions.

The media now is an important player in foreign affairs. An enlightened foreign policy, therefore, must observe all these factors. Only a myopic foreign policy can shut itself in the office and pursue a course that neither sees nor hears beyond the four walls of the South Block. It is important that at the national level as also at the international level the policy makers see beyond themselves.

Since the Helsinki Conference, unfamiliar elements have been influencing world relations. Human rights, till then, pertained to values of compassion, and were never a part of diplomacy. Today environmental concerns and human rights are given priority attention in every foreign office.

On the whole, India has a good record of human rights, though unsavory issues and incidents have occured. An open society like ours is transparent and open to exposures.

We have changed our official response to the Amnesty International whose observations have been given due attention. A democracy must respect and respond to well meaning criticisms from wherever they may emanate. In today's world one must give due attention to ideas—both constructive and critical ones—be these internal or external.

Today Asia, Africa and Latin America are of vital interest to us. So it is imperative that we acquire more knowledge about their history and aspirations in order to enable the South Block to comprehend their policy postures and alignments.

But we know precious little about say Malaysia, Indonesia, Philippines too. Thus we will not be able to evolve our policies realistically. This requires the help and participation of scholars, the think tanks and also universities. In the post-Cold War era, the concepts of the sovereignties of the Nation states are undergoing change despite protestations by some dissenters. Gradually, the powers and the domains of the Nation States are surrendering ground in the Regional Forums. This is inevitable in this era of high technology.

9

Dynamics of Diplomacy*

Ms Barbara Tuckman once wrote,

Each nation, state or a country inhabits a cosmos of its own. It has a cultural tradition; a certain milieu in which it lives, an ambience that it breathes–the product of its own deep historical experience and development; its folklore; its arts and artifacts; its language; its symbolism; its way of thinking and its outlook on life; its prejudices; its hopes and yearnings; its fears and anxieties; its geographical and socio-economic compulsions and coordinates; and also the totality in which its scale of values operates. What is more, many of these elements are not static; they are in a stage of flux undergoing changes.

This is an apt enunciation of the factors that determine the dynamics of a nation's diplomacy. For Indians, the freedom struggle had spelt the course that free India's foreign policy was to follow. Our preferences and alliances were determined by our own historical experiences. Naturally, we had sympathy for those who like us, were victims of the colonizers. Gandhi's struggle

*Speech delivered at the India International Centre on 15/11/1996.

77

against the obnoxious practices of Apartheid in South Africa made the cause of the coloured majority not only a part of our freedom struggle but later, also of our foreign policy.

The British rule here was somewhat different from the style of their governance in the countries of Africa. The slave trade had deprived them of their youth and their cultural legacies, the colonizers had imported the unemployed from Europe and allotted them vast tracks of agricultural lands. The locals were reduced to serfdom. They neither had access to their ancestral properties nor to any education.

For several reasons, the East India Company's methods of exploitation were different. Their textile industry, for instance, could not compete with the highly sophisticated products of Dhaka. Our agricultural lands were heavily loaded, leaving no scope for import of labour. The Raj was keen to imitate the pomp and authority of the Mughals. Architectural features of the Viceregal Lodge, layout of the Mughal Gardens, the Turkish turbans of the attendants and the Viceregal Durbars were aimed at changing our cultural ethos. Economic, military and strategic compulsions made them build some roads, railways and ports to market the industrial goods and facilitate movement of the armed forces. Some visionary men and women in India saw merit in learning the English language and so they established the Anglo-Vedic and Anglo-Islamic schools and colleges.

The enlightened leadership of our freedom struggle, particularly after the end of the 1857 Mutiny, realized that the network of colonizers was widely spread which would require competent opposition. As I have said Gandhi's experiences in South Africa made us partisans in the anti-Apartheid struggle. The Socialist Revolution in the Soviet Union inspired our people also. We were sympathetic to all anti-imperialist and anti-fascist struggles. Nehru projected this feeling by deputing some doctors lead by Dr Kotnis to China and another group to support the anti-fascists in the Spanish Civil War.

As the freedom struggle gained momentum, the contours of our independent foreign policy became discernable. The Congress resolutions articulated that autonomy of choice based on our perceptions of national interests would be the foundation of our diplomacy. Since our liberation and the beginning of the Cold War coincided, the leadership chose to stay away from the rival camps not allowing Washington or Moscow to force us to adhere to them in any way. This was not acceptable to either of the two rival powers. Stalin branded Nehru as 'the running dog of imperialism', while the Americans stigmatized his Non-Alignment as an 'evil'. Here at home, many misperceived it as neutrality.

All through the Cold War, the wise would often tell Nehru that such a policy would end in isolation. This threat continues to haunt us all the time: when we supported the just causes of Vietnam and other countries of Indo-China or when we supported China's entry in the UN. Every time we pursued a policy that would not please the mighty colonizers, we were confronted with such comminations.

End of the Cold War posed some unfamiliar challenges, requiring reorientation of policies within the framework of our basic postulates. I am unhappy to see that even a minor setback in the international fora causes anxiety to those who seek a speedy shift of policies. Of course, the foreign policy should neither be rigid nor dogmatic; the responses must be adjusted to the changes in the national and international environment, keeping in mind our history, legacy, principles and motivations of the others. As per the cliché we must never act out of fear and not be afraid to change if our interests so demand.

In this era, some new factors have entered the world scene. Terrorism in the name of 'Jihad' is an instrument of policies of some nations. We are seeing this in our neighbourhood. I had raised this issue in the UN and with the world powers asking them to respond collectively before it became a menace.

Let me now draw attention to the importance of regional co-operation in the contemporary era. Even mighty powers such as the USA are feeling the need for special relationships with Canada and Mexico. The European Union is an impressive example of the benefits from mutual cooperation. Our foreign policy, there-fore, attached importance not only to the SAARC, but also to the wider neighbourhood in various directions, though SAARC remains its focal point. Unfortunately, the growth of the South Asian cooperation is impinged upon by the myopic policies of Pakistan. However, I continue to hope that the subcontinent will eventually witness such a wholesome regional cooperation as would benefit all. During my tenure as Prime Minister, I had spelt the contours of the 'Gujral Doctrine' that received universal acclaim, wherein India projected a novel concept of non-insistence on point by point reciprocity. This has helped in resolving the lingering water dispute with Bangladesh and infusing trust with the other neighbours. While enunciating the 'Doctrine', I had urged that it would be helpful if the neigh-bouring countries prohibit the use of their territories for any activity that would harm a neighbour. Non-interference in internal affairs of the others is an important component of this percep-tion that also asks all to respect the other's territorial integrity and sovereignty of others and settle disputes, if any, through peaceful bilateral negotiations. These principles, you will agree, would go a long way towards building wholesome neighbourly relationships.

Back in the 1970s, as Ambassador of India in the Soviet Union, I had witnessed the Soviet Union's ill-perceived entry in Afghanistan. All that followed is history now. The Afghan people urgently need an end to their agonies. This can only be possible if the outside powers—particularly the immediate neighbours do not interfere and let them settle their affairs peacefully. To make this plea, during my tenure as Prime Minister, we partici-pated in the Teheran and the New York Conferences. Our offi-cials visited Mazar-e-Sharif and met different segments of the

Afghan polity to convey our point of view. India was willing to extend all humanitarian aid but we were opposed to supply of weapons or making any intervention that would intensify their civil strife. As is known, we recognized the Rabbani regime as the lawful government of Afghanistan and continued to do so.

During my visit to Teheran in 1997, a new chapter of India-Iran relations was opened. The trilateral treaty between India, Iran and Turkmenistan was signed to open a new railway link with Central Asia via Iran and Turkmenstan because the existing circuitous route via Odessa was long and uneconomical.

The Chinese President His Excellency Ziang Jemin had visited India during my tenure as Prime Minister. The talks were warm and friendly and we had jointly taken steps to make the Line of Actual Control more tranquil. Our bilateral trade has expanded and our cultural relations are improving.

The Harare Conference of the G-15 countries brought the leading NAM members closer. It was decided that the G-15 and the ASEAN countries should collaborate in responding to such World Trade Organization (WTO) issues that were averse to the interests of all developing countries. In the name of labour, environment, and human rights non-trade elements were being inducted to impair the interests of all of us.

Relations with the Russian Federation continued with their age-old characteristics. Despite the collapse of the the USSR our friendship with it in its new incarnation as the Russian Federation was wholesome. The political system had changed, but not the geo-strategic realities. Although trade had registered a setback briefly but we have faith in the future of the vast country.

The Indo-US relations, as I have said, are friendly. The volume of trade registered a steady increase and the USA continued to be the largest investor in India—20 per cent of the actual direct inflows come from the USA.

In the end to return to the contending issue of CTBT. We could not sign it for reasons which I have already stated. We have paid the price for safeguarding our security interests. We were denied a temporary seat in the Security Council but we did not relent for reasons which are valid. Once more, it seems, our nerve was being tested and we had to stand up in defence of our interests. The prospect of a permanent seat in the Security Council for India seemed limited since the victors of the last war—that is now half a century old, continue to monopolize the world forums. All the same our policies will continue to courageously defend our interests in the spirit of our legacy. I firmly believe that this great nation of one billion people can never be subdued nor denied its place in the world. We must continue to stand up and uphold our legacy as we have always done.

10

Relevance of the Commonwealth*

We, in South Asia, belong to civilizations dating back to the dawn of history. Our milestones are shared. Our joys are common. For India, it is a matter of pride that it has, in the last half a century, emerged as a self-confident society: united, democratic, secular, and firmly set on the path of modernisation and sustained economic growth.

Our Independence in 1947 acted as the spur to the liberation of over a hundred countries in the post-war era. The principles on which we gained our freedom constituted a turning point in history: a decisive step towards the end of subjugation and colonization, and the beginning of a new world order based on equality, equity and respect for sovereignty.

The Indian Republic chose to remain in the Commonwealth. We did not wish to make the promise of the future a hostage to the rancour of the past. This was our approach, because the principles underlying our freedom struggle were universal: the dignity and equality of human beings. Our fight was against imperialism, not against a people or a country.

The Commonwealth is a voluntary association of sovereign and independent States, bringing together people of many races,

---

*Address at the Opening Ceremony of CHOGM, Edinburg, on 24/10/ 1997.

religions and continents. Amongst its members are the non-aligned and the aligned, the poor and the rich, the North and the South, and the big and the small. Within itself, it represents the widest range of global aspirations. It accommodates differences even as it values consensus.

Over the years, the Commonwealth has evolved. What began as the British Commonwealth was transformed, in 1949, when India joined it, into a free association of independent member nations. At that time, the end to colonialism was in sight, but the process was not yet complete. The years that followed saw the light of freedom illuminate almost every corner of the globe. The process of decolonization was truly complete with the emergence of multi-racial and democratic South Africa in 1994.

At the close of one of the most remarkable centuries, humanity had witnessed, the Commonwealth has entered a third phase, with a clear-cut task before it: to forge a shared vision for the new millennium and the challenges and opportunities that it brings with it.

The twentieth century has witnessed tensions, divisions and wars more brutal than ever before. Yet it has also been a beneficial age. Some 200 nations are free today, aspiring to be equal partners with an equal voice in shaping the destiny of humanity. The boundaries of human possibility have expanded manifold, and men and women around the world live longer and fuller lives today than ever in the past.

Even so, can we forget that human history has, for too long, been one of war and oppression, punctuated with brief intervals of peace and freedom? This really is the challenge of the times, of strengthening peace, the freedom, and the spirit and essence of a global brotherhood that post-war institutions such as the Commonwealth represent.

How does one ensure a just ordering of relations amongst nations, so that the interests of one are seen in harmony with the interests of the world community at large? Can we make global democracy credible? How do we overcome narrow nationalisms and learn that, ultimately, it is in giving that we gain, in sharing that we grow, and only in serving a larger good that we really serve ourselves? These are issues statesmanship today must address.

Shortly after assuming responsibility as India's first Prime Minister, Jawaharlal Nehru observed, and I quote:

> I have become more and more convinced that so long as we do not recognize the supremacy of moral law in our national and international relations, we shall have no enduring peace. So long as we do not adhere to the right means, the end will not be right and fresh evils will flow from it. That was the essence of Gandhi's message, and humankind will have to appreciate it in order to see and act clearly.

Can we in the Commonwealth take a lead in defining an international ethic, a morality such as we seek to practice in our personal lives, of treating others as we would wish ourselves to be treated; a world where honour is respected, where truth and natural justice prevail?

Trade, finance and technology have brought people closer to each other than ever before, even when their objectives are vastly different. Many developing countries are being asked to adjust to this process of globalization at a pace and in conditions that are not of their own choosing. Equal opportunity, and democracy—ideals which we all share—are often absent in the restricted chambers of the international economic system. And yet, I have little doubt that, in the long run, globalization will succeed only if it is equitable and just and is so seen by the vast majority of mankind.

The institutional systems that oversee the globalized economy must reflect an enlightened balance of interests. India and many developing countries are in the process of economic reform and restructuring. Their commitment to social and redistributive justice needs to be understood and appreciated. The developing countries of today will become the high growth economic frontiers of tomorrow. If today they are not provided better terms of trade and market access, and greater resources for their critical developmental needs, the consequences will adversely affect overall global prosperity tomorrow.

It is my conviction that the Commonwealth can and must be made an instrument of cooperation that has direct relevance for vital issues of economic growth of developing member countries. This body can and must become an effective interlocutor between the North and the South. The Commonwealth can and must strive for greater democracy and equity in global economic decision making. The Commonwealth can and must ensure that all its members share the benefits of technology.

As we look ahead, there are some other issues that will need special attention. I have in mind, in particular, the menace of terrorism and the scourge of international drug trade.

Terrorism and drug trafficking are often tied together, and both have a link with yet another global menace, moneylaundering. Together, these issues threaten international peace, stability and security. Terrorism is indiscriminate in its impact, affecting entire communities, and open democracies in particular are areas vulnerable to it. We need an effective global strategy to deal with these problems. It is with this end in view that I had mooted the idea of a Universal Extradition Treaty that would enable the international community to pursue the perpetrators of these crimes across national frontiers, and ensure that they do not seek or obtain refuge in any part of the world.

The problems of the present, if left unresolved, will assume the nature of a crisis in the future. We stand at the watershed of history. All of us are responsible for ensuring that in our meetings, dialogue leads to action and goodwill leads to results. The onus is on us to ensure that this unique forum, which we have the honour and privilege to belong, distinguishes itself in the present millennium as a real bridge between the needs and opportunities of all its members.

In India, our ancient sages believed in the motto:

Vasudaiva Kutumbakam

The World is one family

The Commonwealth is both a symbol of this belief and the hope that it will be fulfilled.

11

Peace, Prosperity and Social Justice*

Ours is an ancient civilization. In these last fifty years, the culture of this country has been enriched further and this in itself reflects unity and secularism. Our country is moving towards modernity while keeping its heritage intact. There is a certain attraction in this land whereby people belonging to different cultures and languages have been able to mingle freely and enrich our civilization.

Partition and Menace of Communalism

On 15 August 1947, while on the one hand in the Central Hall of the Parliament the country was looking towards the future with hope, on the other, it was witness to the menace of communalism at its worst in areas like Punjab and Bengal which were partitioned. In the name of religion, innocent people were being slaughtered, women were being openly humiliated and barbarism was at its peak. Millions of men and women, old and young and children including myself, were crossing the border from both sides with tears in their eyes and a smile on their lips, with

---

*Free renderings in English of the former Prime Minister, Shri IK Gujral's address to the nation delivered in Hindi from the ramparts of Red Fort on the 50th Anniversary of India's Independence and on the 51st Independence Day on 15/8/1997.

no hope for the future and darkness behind. I was also a part of a group travelling from Pakistan to India and I recall that even during this painful hour, we remembered Gandhi who inspired us and showed us the path of a secular democratic India even while putting his life at stake. It was assumed and later confirmed by posterity that had if we had chosen some other path, the country could not have stayed united or progressed.

Ours is a country of diversities. We follow different religions and speak different languages. Quite often our eating habits and lifestyles also vary. We have witnessed diverse aspects of history for the last several centuries. The struggle for Independence has united all these diversities into a firm chain. The slogan Unity in Diversity has been firmly inscribed in our hearts. Every word of this meant sacrifice, patriotism and a firm faith in destiny.

Gandhi raised a unique army of soldiers who had no weapons and were forbidden from even talking about violence. This was a new definition of valour. People's faith in Gandhi led lawyers to give up practice, students to leave their schools and colleges and they started filling up jails. Farmers left their fields and labourers their factories. In these last days of the struggle, things came to such a peak that the youth working with the Indian Navy also rebelled. The country was witnessing a new kind of revolt. The roots of imperialism were shaken in the face of this struggle.

I take pride in this fact and I wish to reiterate that the freedom was won by the people of this country—it was not gifted to them. It is for a reason that when the Constitution of India was framed, its opening lines read, 'We, the people of India give to ourselves this Constitution.' This constitution and this great country gave us a democracy and fundamental rights which enshrined equality of religion, caste, creed and gender and it is under this democratic system that crores of people exercised their franchise in the 9th general election, a shining example of the largest democracy of the world. Gradually, the African and Asian nations started attaining freedom. British imperialism started losing ground after India's Independence and we witnessed the last chapter of British imperialism closing recently in Hong Kong.

Gandhi's Dream Fulfilled

When Gandhi dreamt of India's future, he had said that the country will attain real freedom only on the day when a dalit would become the President of this country. In the person of Shri KR Narayanan, we have been able to fulfil the dream of the Mahatma. Our outgoing President, of whom the whole country is proud of, is from a very poor and downtrodden family and has endowed the Rashtrapati Bhawan with a new pride and respect. It is a matter of further happiness that the President has a very high place among the intellectuals of this country. This is a feather in the cap of our democracy that the backward sections of the society today are attaining their rightful place. All the countrymen today, whether they are from the minorities, scheduled castes or scheduled tribes—are working unitedly for the development of the country.

Women constitute an important part of our society. Our religions and cultures put women on a very high pedestal, but I am constrained to say, with a sense of sorrow and regret that our politics, apparently, is hesitating in giving women a place of equality. There was a revolution sometime back in the Panchayati Raj elections, when about one lakh women rightfully became the leaders of panchayats and municipal corporations. When I go to any city and meet the lady Mayor or the lady Sarpanch, I feel very happy and proud. In this I also see a glorious future for India. These days we are trying, and I want to reiterate the promise which I made in the Parliament, to give women their rightful place in the country's politics. We must remember that unless this is achieved no society or country can progress. Women should get their equal place in every field whether in the political, economic or social arena.

Protecting the Girl Child

It is very unfortunate that even today in some Indian families, when a girl child is born, the family at large feels unhappy. Unfortunately, some families abort female foetus's when they learn about it in advance. My government formulated two policies to stop this menace. The first was that doctors were legally prohibited from revealing the sex of the child in the womb. The second policy was perhaps more important, where the government would provide financial help to the families to whom a girl child is born, if they were living below the poverty line. Later, scholarships would be awarded when the girl child starts going to school.

I appeal to all countrymen and political and social institutes and also to those women who have been elected to the Panchayats to work unitedly to change the atmosphere in the country so that small girls are looked after well. They should get a full opportunity to blossom and men and women should have an equal place in society.

I would also like to say that whether they are boys or girls, unless and until our future generations go to school, the society cannot make further progress. My government acceded the right to education as a fundamental right for every child and we presented the amendment bill in Parliament. The next scheme was to open more schools and raise the standard of education. Our country will have a bright future only when every child below 14 years will be able to go to school every morning wearing a colourful uniform. Children should not be deprived of childhood joys and forced into labour. That is why, I want to emphasize that all of us should contribute our mite in this endeavour of the government.

91

Fight Against Corruption

Corruption is eating into the vitals of the country. The country is in greater danger from those who occupy higher offices and betray the nation by accepting bribes. If the country's enemies attack us from outside, our gallant army is capable of facing them and they put their lives at stake in the most difficult circumstances. But if somebody from inside becomes a traitor by accepting bribes and betrays the nation, he creates a greater danger to the country. Corruption is rampant everywhere. It seems that whether it is a matter of government purchases, paying of taxes, or paying of customs duties, some people think that corruption is their birthright.

It is all the more unfortunate that common men face more difficulties because of petty corrupt practices. Even the slightest of work cannot be completed without bribing somebody, whether it is a police station, a village patwari, municipality, an electric station, a telephone department or the revenue department. The sin of corruption is prevalent everywhere. The common people especially the poor and the middle classes suffer the most. On several occasions, I have seen this feeling of helplessness written large on their faces.

The nexus between corruption and politics has taken a turn for the worse today when criminals are entering politics. When I see the dark clouds ahead, I feel more determined to eliminate this challenge of corruption. All of us will have to work unitedly to eradicate corruption. The government alone will not be able to achieve this goal.

The first thing which we have to do is to implement electoral reforms which have been discussed for a long time now. Some work has been done in this regard but that is not enough and perhaps we will not be able to meet the objectives within the stipulated timeframe. Corruption will prevail till the day money is collected in the name of fighting elections. Therefore, complete reforms are imperative. The second thing towards which we must draw our attention is the criminalization of politics. Criminals are aligning themselves with the political parties and we must break this nexus with courage and determination. I honestly believe that every political party, finds fault with the others but overlooks its own greater faults. If a *goonda* belongs to the other political party, we consider him a *goonda* but if he belongs to our party, we make him sit by our side and give him respect and regard. Legally, we have to meet this challenge but simultaneously I call upon all political parties to do some soul searching. This is the biggest challenge before politics and the politician, today, if he has to become the leader of tomorrow.

Bribe takers should not be allowed to escape the law but we, who are compelled to offer bribes, should take a pledge and start a new type of Satyagraha, non-cooperation, and assert that we would not give bribes whatever be the difficulties and delays. It will be a new form of Satyagraha. This Satyagraha can take us very far. Today we do not have any leader of the stature of Mahatma Gandhi. But all of us can unitedly achieve this objective. The philosophy of Gandhi continues to inspire us to form committees in localities, villages and cities to help each other so that those who give and take bribes come out of this compulsion. I don't know whether some of you remember this or not. I have seen this with my own eyes that when Gandhi had started the Salt Satyagraha, people had inquired that how was it possible to remove imperialism by making salt. I recall that when my father decided to join the Salt Satyagraha, his fellow lawyers told him that 'you are a literate person, whereas Gandhi is an old man and he has lost his senses'. They used to ask if it were possible to make British imperialism give way by making salt. But Gandhi had confidence in himself. He was a farsighted man, people followed him. The issue which had started from a handful of salt ended with the end of British rule.

There was a time when accepting bribes would have lead to social boycott. It was a matter of great insult if anybody associated with someone who accepted bribes. All of us should work unitedly to create an atmosphere in this society, which would emphasise that we do not vote for the corrupt, we do not keep any kind of relationship with any criminal and we do not give any respect to such persons in society.

The struggle for India's independence achieved success when the youth joined in. There was enthusiasm in that commitment which along with the will to sacrifice, led the nation to freedom. Today once again I call upon you to join this new struggle against corruption. There are some aspects of corruption which relate to government policies. My government took a decision that whenever there was a big government purchase, whether it was for defence or some other department, its procedure had to be very transparent so that people did not have doubts about it. We created a committee to approve the purchases of arms and fighter planes and other defence equipment. The members of this committee were people of the highest integrity. Such committees should be formed in all ministries and departments who make large purchases. This committee should work in an open way so that people can see that there are no kickbacks involved. There should be nothing in it which even in the slightest measure smells of corruption.

Right to Information

During my tenure as Prime Minister, we gave the Right to Information to our people through a new law. Under this Right, every citizen would possess the right to seek information on any of the Official Secrecy Acts. I also advised the Chief Ministers to form special courts to expeditiously deal with corruption cases. This is a very important task and I have urged to the Supreme Court to help us in punishing the corrupt.

My government formed a National Commission which rec-ommended abolition of outdated laws which are not required now and suggested reforms in the present laws to ensure early settlement of cases in courts. The Civil Code and the Penal Code should also be changed so that cases do not remain in the court files for years on end.

Common Minimum Programme

The Indian community today is emerging as a big economic giant before the world after the hard work of fifty long years. Earlier, even a needle to sew clothes used to be imported. I recall that before partition, there was a very rich businessman in Karachi who made a big fortune by importing needles. Today, when we take a look at our industries and factories, we raise our heads with pride on our achievements in these fifty years.

We attained political freedom more than half a century ago and today, we are marching forward towards economic free-dom. Our schemes have lead the country towards the goal of economic independence. These long years of hard work of our countrymen have borne fruit. Today, the world considers India as a very big market not only for purchasing goods but also for the marketing of our industrial products. Our labourers and farm-ers are taking the country on the path of economic progress by dint of their hard work. No country in the world today can remain isolated. The United Front Government formulated a Common Minimum Programme. This programme was multifac-eted and our effort was to touch upon those sectors of the economy where some kind of stalemate has crept in.

In the last fifty years this country has striven to set up a large number of Public Sector Units (PSUs). I paid special attention to the Public Sector and where there was earlier talk of closing down ten big Public Sector companies, they were revived in my

95

tenure as Prime Minister. My policy was to infuse the Public Sector with fresh life so that the country increases its wealth along with the people's prosperity.

Rapid Economic Growth

Today, whether it is Delhi or outside, within the country or the city, new roads need to be built. Industries have to increase, for which infrastructural issues like power, post and telegraph and telecommunications need to be addressed. Unless we do so, our economy may not be able to progress. That was the reason behind the United Front Government's focus and stress on these issues.

If we strive and aspire together, with the efforts of labourers and farmers, our growth rate should move upwards. Ours is primarily an agricultural economy. The real strength of the country is the farmer, his effort and production. In the last fifty years, our foodgrains production has increased four times. Import of foodgrains for people is a thing of the past. Our population has increased tremendously but I am grateful to the farmer for making us self-sufficient in foodgrains. Our country has experienced both the Green and White Revolutions. Due to the White Revolution, India today is the world's biggest producer of milk. Our current focus is on improving agricultural production. That is why, areas that receive scanty rainfall need special attention. In areas where agriculture is totally dependent on rainfall and dryland farming the stress should be on improving agricultural production by using science and technology. We have to do a lot for the hard working farmers, so we must lay special emphasis on the welfare of agricultural labour especially landless labourers. Since they are backward and in live extreme poverty, there is need for their insurance so that in case of the bread earner's sad demise, the family members do not lack succour.

Garibi Hatao—A Reality

The slogan *Garibi Hatao* was coined a long time back. The task before my Government was how to translate it into reality. I had said that in our agricultural economy around 60 to 65 per cent of people remained dependent on agriculture. It is with extreme sadness that I say that the land reforms have not been implemented honestly. Our country cannot progress unless the people who actually work on the fields get the land. Therefore, I urged especially those states where land reforms had not been implemented to stress on this and to formulate such a programme which within the next one or two years would translate this into reality. Poverty and illiteracy are two sides of the same coin and they should be eradicated. The welfare of the labourer and poor classes should be promoted not only by supporting agriculture but also by setting up of cottage and small scale industries. Unemployment especially amongst the educated unemployed needs to be addressed. It has only one solution and that is economic progress and advancement. Eradication of illiteracy is another essential ingredient for the development of the country. The nation cannot progress as long as its people are illiterate. Somebody has once said and I would like to quote 'tell me one country where people are literate and the country is backward and tell me one country where people are illiterate and the country has moved forward.'

I remember the days when I was in college and Gandhi had raised the slogan of 'each one teach one'. The country would benefit greatly if each person—whether he is studying, working in an office or doing some job in the village—decided to teach one illiterate person in a year. There are some states in our country which have experienced this revolution. We can talk of Kerala, Andhra Pradesh, Mizoram and Tamil Nadu to a great extent, areas where we have grappled with illiteracy successfully and it has resulted in decreasing population growth rate. An educated woman contributes greatly in this mission. If an edu-

97

cated woman understands how the growing population can be stopped, how families can be kept small, the setback to our development posed by population explosion can be checked.

The Green Revolution in our country was the direct result of effective application of science and technology. It is a matter of pride that thanks to our scientists we can both make and launch our satellites. There is a new future for the youth of today and science and technology and computers have shown them a new path. I recall Jawaharlal Nehru's statement that it is not enough for everyone to become a scientist or technologist, it is more important to inculcate a scientific temper among our children and youth. When a child switches on an electric bulb and asks how it functions he should not be scolded. He should be made to understand how electricity is produced and used. When a child acquires a questioning spirit, scientific temper is created and it will eliminate the era of superstitions.

Long ago, Lord Buddha had said that the people should not have blind faith in anything. 'Do not believe because I am saying so. Also do not believe what it is written in a book.' Question everything—what, why, how, when, these questions if raised, would change our thought process and the country will progress. Today I am proud to share with you that in 1987, this country had pledged its gold to import petrol; in 1997, we had three thousand crore dollars as our foreign exchange reserve. This is our hard earned money. Our businessmen have earned it. Our industrialists have earned it. Our exporters have earned it and a large portion of it has come from the people who closely watch the economic developments and invest when they find their capital adequately safe. A substantial contribution has also come from non-resident Indians.

Hoping for a Bright Future

We all envisage a new future for the country. I am reminded of

Gandhi's statement which said that he would consider the country to be free when he can wipe the tears from every eye. It is true that we have wiped some tears. But we cannot honestly say that today there are no tears in the eyes of our millions. Today, therefore, the major issue before us is how to eradicate poverty—the poverty of scheduled castes, scheduled tribes and those below the poverty line, irrespective of their religion or faith. So we need to lay special emphasis on such programmes and plans. As I have mentioned earlier, at the time of Independence, our population was thirty-two crores and in these fifty years it has increased three folds. We have to give special attention to those who still remain below the poverty line. We have to try and control the growing population and there are very strong reasons for this. The biggest reason is poverty. Illiteracy and low status of women also lead to an increase in population.

Anti-Pollution Campaign

My attention is drawn to slums where people live in extremely unhygienic surroundings. Similarly, pollution, which is harming the health of our children, is a cause for concern. Some years ago, I had visited Sweden. At that time, we felt that poverty alone breeds pollution. Now we see our country falling into a vicious circle. On the one hand, pollution breeds poverty and on the other hand prosperous people are causing greater pollution. Their cars emit smoke. They do not pay attention to this and do not object to accumulation of filth in their surroundings. Therefore, if we all do not come together and try to break this vicious circle; if we do not fight against pollution the country will not be rid of filth and disease. The government has framed a lot of policies for cleaning the rivers and lakes. These policies have succeeded to an extent but a lot of work still remains to be done. I emphasize that if the government keeps cleaning rivers and we keep polluting them, the purpose will be defeated. So we should awaken the people to implement anti-pollution campaigns and see to it that industries do not emit pollutants. Fertilizers and insecticides should not be used in such a way that the ground water is polluted and it becomes difficult to get clean drinking water. This is why there is a shortage of clean drinking water. Though we have had a comprehensive environment policy, my top most priority and foremost challenge in the 9th Plan was to provide clean drinking water to everyone.

National Commission for Safai Karamcharis

The weaker sections of the society especially the *safai karamcharis* are today one of the most backward sections of the society. They have been denied social justice so far. My Government had set up a National Commission for *safai karamcharis*, to look into their plight. The Government also tried to remove the stigma attached to night soil workers. Our attention was especially focussed on *safai karamcharis*. So that they achieve economic independence. This independence will come when people from the backward classes; attain a place of respect in society.

The Gujral Doctrine

I wish to spend a few minutes on India's foreign policy. Its foundations were laid during our freedom struggle by Mahatma Gandhi and Jawaharlal Nehru. About Gandhi, it is always said that he was born in India, but his political birth took place in Africa. When our Independence came fifty years ago, it was said that the winds of change would also sweep Africa and the rest of Asia. And indeed, soon, one by one the countries of Africa and Asia threw off the yoke of colonialism. These new independent nations came together to create an organisation called NAM. Our foreign policy was initiated by Jawaharlal Nehru. He said 'An independent nation's foreign policy should always be independent'. That is why India has never been a part of any bloc. When the world was divided into various blocs, India made sure that it did not get involved in bloc politics. We are proud of our Non-Aligned foreign policy.

I refused to sign the CTBT and even today, we remain firm on this issue. We will not sign any such treaty under pressure and until the nuclear weapon states destroy their stockpiles.

I can proudly say that I have given a new direction to our foreign policy. This policy has been referred to by the media and intellectuals as the Gujral doctrine. Under the doctrine, we wished to improve relations with our neighbours and we are progressing towards this. But we have to keep one thing in mind, that while relations can be improved we should not compromise on our security and national interest. Our armed forces have proved many a time that they can defend the nation if faced by an outside threat. Our history is testimony to the fact that we have never lost in wars because we did not have the state of the art weapons. If our opponent had canons we fought with swords and this was a mismatch. Our soldiers died displaying the highest bravery, while our women folk would commit *jauhar* or sati. I promised our Navy, Air Force and Army that they would not remain technologically backward and they could face the enemy eye to eye. Our scientists and technologists are today able to produce weapons which we do not have to buy from abroad. The Cold War has ended. Inimical forces are becoming friendly. Therefore, our foreign policy lays stress on regional cooperation with countries in South Asia.

We have witnessed development of new friendly relations with Bangladesh. Our relations with Sri Lanka also improved and our traditional relationship with Nepal has been further rejuvenated. New levels of friendship were established with the States of Myanmar and Maldives and an environment of friendliness was emerging. We raised the concept of regional cooperation.

During of my tenure as Prime Minister, Nagaland started its march towards peace. A ceasefire was achieved after 30 years of militancy. And I hope that in the days to come, peace would be restored in the entire Northeastern region. But one thing should be clear to all of us that there would be no compromise with terrorism. People using arms will be strictly dealt with. The country is eager to welcome back the misguided youths. They are our brethren and children and if they give up arms and ask for their right, we will ensure that they get them.

Indo-Pak friendship would benefit the two countries. It will, in fact, benefit the entire South-East region and would enable the seven nations in the region to establish a common front against poverty and backwardness. I want to state on behalf of India that we want to establish good friendly relations with the countries of the region including Pakistan. But we must accept that friendly relations can be established only when we do not interfere in the internal affairs of each other and territorial sovereignty of each country is honoured. Today, India has the capability to protect its national independence, and there would be no compromise on secular unity and integrity. We want friendship without endangering our territorial integrity.

Our foreign policy led to further improvement of relations with neighbouring countries. Our relationship with the countries of Asia and Africa, Russia, Japan, China and Korea have improved. The relationship with China is also improving. We also witnessed the emergence of a better relationship with the European powers. European powers are today making heavy investments in our country. Our relations with the Americans are old and friendly. Our economic ties with America have been strengthened and we intend to further improve them.

Our war against corruption should be wholehearted, honest and candid and for this we have to build a massive movement in which all of us can join hands so that corruption, both in politics and also in public life ends. And at the same time, this

movement must focus on small-time corruption, in police sta-
tions, in villages, in government offices where we must start a
new type of Satyagraha, i.e. non-cooperation with the ones who
are corrupt; refusing to give into corruption. It needs courage.
Sometimes, it is difficult but it is daring. Gandhi's main heritage
is that non-cooperation can achieve wonders. Let us achieve it
once again.

We Indians following different religions speaking different
languages, living in different parts of India and having different
historical divisions, are one.

So let us come together and pledge to build a nation which
will be united inspite of its diversities. We will follow our faith,
our own religions but will remain united. We will end all existing class differences. We will build a nation where there will be
no lower class or upper class, a nation where women will be
honoured and they will get their due status. We shall make a
country, a country of equals; a country which is socially just; a
country where women can demand their rights and where the
scheduled castes and scheduled tribes and minorities occupy a
place of primacy.

II

THE GUJRAL DOCTRINE

(L-R) Mr Satish Gujral, Pandit Nehru and Mr IK Gujral

IK Gujral being sworn in as Prime Minister on 21 April 1997

The Prime Minister and Mrs Gujral with the Speaker of the South African
Parliament Frene Ginwala and children, Cape Town; October 1997

With the President of South Africa Nelson Mandela, Cape Town; October 1997

Mrs and Mr Gujral with President Nelson Mandela and
Mrs Graca Machel Mandela

The Prime Minister and Mrs Gujral with the Pope John Paul II,
Rome; September 1997

With Queen Elizabeth II and the Duke of Edinburgh, New Delhi; October 1997

Greeting Hillary Clinton, wife of the then US President Bill Clinton,
at the funeral of Mother Teresa, Calcutta; September 1997

With Mr Kofi Annan at the UN General Assembly Session; September 1997

IK Gujral presiding over the UN General Assembly

Heads of Government of Commonwealth nations with
Queen Elizabeth II, Edinburgh; October 1997.

IK Gujral addressing the Heads of State at the opening session of the Commonwealth Heads of Government Meet (CHOGM), Edinburgh; October 1997.

IK Gujral addressing the UNDP Regional Millennium Meeting
for Asia and the Pacific, Seoul; November 1998

With Pakistani Foreign Minister Gohar Ayub Khan, New Delhi; 1997

With former Pakistani Prime Minister Nawaz Sharif, New York; September 1997

Visit of Prime Minister IK Gujral to Dhaka in January 1998; with
Prime Minister Sheikh Hasina Wajed

Prime Minister IK Gujral meeting King Birendra of Nepal in June 1997

IK Gujral with the Prime Minister of Sri Lanka, Chandrika Kumaratunga

With President Bill Clinton in New York; September 1997

With British Prime Minister Tony Blair, Edinburgh; October 1997

With the President of Russia Boris Yeltsin and Prime Minister Primakov (on his right), Moscow; March 1997

IK Gujral with Willey Brandt, the former Chancellor of Germany

With President of France, Jacques Chirac at the official reception
at Rashtrapati Bhawan 25 January 1998

In conversation with Egyptian President Hosni Mubarak, Cairo;
October 1997

IK Gujral with President of Tanzania,
His Excellency Mr. Benjamin William Mkapa

Prime Minister IK Gujral with President Yoweri Kaguta Museveni of Uganda,
Kampala; October 1997

Shri IK Gujral with Saddam Hussein, 1990

Prime Minister IK Gujral addressing the gathering at the Red Fort on
Independence Day; 15 August 1997

12

Significance of an Independent
Foreign Policy*

Peace, nuclear disarmament, self-reliance, Non-Alignment and economic development are the bedrock on which India's foreign policy has continued to rest. Its main source of strength is the continually-evolving national consensus. The legacy of our freedom struggle gives it a historical perspective and a sense of direction.

The latter part of the twentieth century inducted new elements that have invariably influenced diplomacies of all nations. Terrorism, drug trafficking, conservation of environment and promotion of the human rights now occupy a central position on the world stage. Nations take their own time to respond and adjust to these challenges; India is no exception. We have our own views about the emerging world order that must be made socially just and equitable. At the same time, our legacy beckons us to preserve the Independence of our foreign policy, judging every issue on its merit and keeping in mind our national interests.

From the day of its birth as an independent Nation State, India was resolutely opposed to all alignments that divided the

---

*Speech delivered at the Rajendra Prasad Academy on 14/10/1996.

world into camps. The end of the Cold War has to a great extent reduced tensions and opened new vistas of cooperation.

Despite all the dramatic changes, I am unable to say that a 'new dawn' of peace and cooperation has arrived. Aggressive and exclusivist sentiments continue to tear apart the social fabric with disastrous consequences for development, peace and stability. A loose political concert continues to exercise military, economic, technological hegemony, while the voice of the developing world is marginalized. In these circumstances, the Non-Aligned Movement (NAM) acquires added importance for collectively safeguarding interests of the Third World.

Widespread terrorism cum fundamentalism poses a major threat to stability. It deprives innocent citizens of their right to life. Built on narrow outlooks that are anathema to liberal and democratic values, they pose a formidable challenge to civil societies. While exploiting openness and the freedom offered by democratic societies, they exploit and undermine them. As the G-7's Lyon Declaration said, 'the terrorist does not respect any social order or civilizational heritage'.

Thanks to shortening of distances and instant communications, the world today is truly a global village. Keeping this in mind, my government accorded priority attention to her immediate neighbours to promote peace and stability in the region, and for development of stronger economic relations. I visited almost all the countries in our subcontinent, soon after assuming charge as Prime Minister. We wished Pakistan stability and prosperity and with this in mind, proposed the resumption of Foreign Secretary level dialogue to address all issues of mutual concern on the basis of the Simla Agreement.

We attached the greatest importance to our relations with our neighbours. I have already stated that five basic principles of the Gujral Doctrine, which guided our relations with our immediate neighbours. These principles were first, India does not seek reciprocity but gives all that it can in good faith and trust. Second, no South Asian country should allow the use of its territory against the interest of a fellow country in the region. Third, that none would interfere in the internal affairs of the other. Fourth, all of us in South Asia must respect each other's territorial integrity and sovereignty. And finally, we would settle all disputes through peaceful bilateral negotiations. These five principles or a 'new Panchsheel' or the Gujral Doctrine—if scrupulously adhered, are bound to achieve a fundamental recasting of the regional relationships including, I venture to say, radical change in the tormented relationship between India and Pakistan, in a friendly, and cooperative mould.

China is our important and largest neighbour involving our economic and security interests. Both of us decided to delink the final settlement of the boundary issue from the need to reinforce friendly relations. A number of Confidence Building Measures are now in place along the Line of Control. Sustained friendship between India and China will lay a durable foundation for a peaceful and prosperous Asia.

Geography has determined our historic and close relations with the countries of the Association of South East Asian Nations (ASEAN). With Myanmar joining its membership, we now share a nearly 1600-mile long border with this Association of ten sovereign countries. As stated before, our 'Sectoral dialogue Partnership' of 1992 was upgraded to a 'Full dialogue partnership' with the ASEAN.

India played a pioneering role in the consolidation of the 'Indian Ocean Rim Association' which includes countries of the three continents: Australia, Africa and Asia. When fully operationalized, this could become a very large common market in the world.

Europe—both the East and the West—has been our traditional associates. We have supported the political and economic integration of Europe. The annual Troika meetings between the European Union (EU) and India have been very beneficial. We have also concluded the third generation agreement with the European Union. At the same time, our bilateral commercial relations with all countries of Europe remains satisfactory.

India's long and cherished relations with the Russian Federation bear a hallmark of beneficial friendship and cooperation, based on mutual trust and confidence. Both of us have adjusted with the changed circumstances in Russia and the countries comprising the Commonwealth of the erstwhile Soviet Union. Their market economies give a more independent role to private enterprise, making our commercial interactions smoother.

India's economic reforms programmes had a positive impact on Indo-US economic relations. Our bilateral trade had increased by 19 per cent with a turnover of nearly US$ 9 billion. As of 1996, the US companies accounted for over one-third (38 per cent) of the foreign investment commitments in India, and almost 20 per cent of the actual direct investments. The positive economic trends were sometimes lost in the cacophony of occasional differences—such as over the Comprehensive Nuclear Test Ban Treaty, that got an inordinate amount of media attention. However, we hoped that with the goodwill and mutual respect that we shared, there was no reason why we should not be able to overcome any ephemeral differences.

As I have stated before, India continues to oppose discriminatory and partial measures of arms control such as the CTBT and the NPT. India joined 27 Non-Aligned and neutral countries, at the Conference on Disarmament, to present a phased programme for elimination of nuclear weapons by the year 2020. This still remains on the international agenda but without any promise from the five Nuclear Weapon Powers.

Another important element which has a bearing on our foreign policy is the Indian Diaspora, created out of both forced migration as indentured labour during the colonial era, and voluntary migration in the more recent times. Handsome contributions made by the Indian Diaspora to their adopted countries as also to India have been well documented. While involved in the economic growth and social development of their host countries, they retain their links with India. They can be an important source of technological know-how and investments. Their remittances, particularly of the short-term Indian workers in the Gulf and other countries are a significant source of foreign exchange for our country. Our foreign policy must strengthen these relations, while ensuring that our actions do not in any way impinge on the sovereignty of the host countries. We have to keep these governments informed about the role and propaganda by few misguided extremist elements in the Indian Diaspora.

In conclusion, I must say that India's foreign policy represents continuity and faith in the moral principles. We have retained these paradigms while responding pragmatically to past and emerging challenges, and to the changing global scenario. The primary interest of our foreign policy has been to safeguard our national interests—but not in the narrow and selfish sense. We have unflinchingly supported causes that were dear to us ranging from elimination of Apartheid to supporting the Vietnamese struggle. Some might talk in loose terms of India being isolated on one particular issue or the other. India is a big country of over 96 crore people. We cannot be isolated. We firmly believe in the ideal of the world coming closer together and ultimately realizing the ideal of One World.

We are a fairly young independent Nation State, though a very ancient civilization. Therefore, our foreign policy has gradually evolved, acquiring greater substance while responding to various challenges. We are securely moored in the framework of an inalienable perspective, that of the Panchsheel, Non-Alignment, developing friendly relations with all, and retaining an enlightened self-interest.

13

The Spirit of NAM*

I believe that the fates of South Asian countries are so inter-twined that their survival and development can be possible and profitable only through cooperation.

In this era of global change, old alignments are yielding to new arrangements that may not be always palatable but their appraisal and understanding has to be the first task before any foreign policy.

The Cold War was fought by two mutually-antagonistic 'international cultures'. A systematic global change has ended these agonizing confrontations. With the receding of tension between the two mutually-antagonistic power blocks, we now witness an emerging pattern of cooperation-cum-competition between their individual members.

If Non-Alignment looks like a scattered force during this transition, it is because it is yet to recast itself for a new international role. It was in this context that I had proposed to my Yugoslav counterpart, Mr Loncer, in 1990, to convene an informal meeting of international foreign officials to collectively apply their minds to emerging challenges.

The NAM has, often in the past, intervened to safeguard peace and push back the colonial and racially-biased regimes.

*Lecture delivered at the Naval War College, Bombay on 5/12/1991.

Contemporary situation demands that we collectively work our regimes to release ourselves from debt traps and economic degenerations. The IMF and World Bank prescriptions are further tightening the noose. Breathers, if at all, provide only short-lived relief.

The crisis in which we find ourselves entrapped is not inevitable. It is not a product of forces beyond our control. Faulty and gross mismanagement of economies on one hand and myopic security perceptions on the other have caused it.

The NAM—in spirit of trust and cooperation—should initiate a process of evolving systems and attitudes to end regional wars and tension amongst neighbours.

This may seem a gigantic and impossible task but some countries of Europe have already shown the way by burying old hatchets. Why can't we do it? NAM should also address itself to the task of changing the role and structure of the UN, that is being increasingly used, or may one say, misused by the rich and the powerful to advance their own interests.

Any 'New Vision of the Future' has to inevitably spell out, as done by Nehru in the 1950s, principles that would require democratisation of the World bodies: the UN; Security Council, World Bank, IMF, GATT, etc. Today, the security of all nations—big or small—inevitably implies economic development of all nations.

Two villains have entered the international scene: Terrorism and Drug trafficking. The two are acting in nexus and sometimes acquire state support and even sponsorship. An open arms bazaar facilitates their activity. Unless these are curbed by collective action they are bound to destabilize all societies. Even those who may be deriving temporary benefit from their nefarious activities stand to lose eventually.

The evolution of an equitable environmental regime is another issue of vital interest to all South Asian countries. At present, the dice is loaded in favour of powerful industrialized nations.

Unless we act in unison we may be denied access to the latest technology and left to languish in dungeons of backwardness. Isn't it time that we in the SAARC undertook such an exercise to collectively corelate ourselves with the changing world?

'No South Asian Country should allow the use of its territory against the interest of another.' As Foreign Minister, I had espoused this principle and further promised that India would abide by this and never commit its forces outside its territory except in self-defence. I view the principle of self-determination positively since in all developing countries, the polity is over centralized and there is a heavy deficit of self-determination even when political systems are democratic. Self-determination or participation in Self-Government must begin at the grassroot level through democratically-elected village councils and cover the entire political society. Elections must, of course, be free and fair and to establish their credibility a team of eminent persons from SAARC should, as a practice, be invited to monitor the process.

Self-determination, however, must not be perceived to disturb national boundaries, as doing so would engage neighbours in prolonged and agonizing mutual hostility, bloodshed and resource drainage.

We see a mushrooming of regional, sub-national and even communal identities all over the world, including Europe. This sometimes strains inter-state relations and inhibits regional cooperation for peace, security and development.

It is time, I would suggest, that South Asian leaders and opinion makers engage themselves in free, open-minded discussions to build a regional consensus on a stated basic principle that must govern South Asian relationships.

Any framework of such a consensus must keep in mind that South Asia has been slow in imbibing the post-Cold War chemistry of cooperation. Our outmoded mindsets and faulty security concepts do not permit us to take a holistic view of security.

Deeply ingrained suspicions of the neighbours result in ever increasing expense on military hardware, that in turn, intensifies economic distress, internal disturbances and creates enhanced need for outside help and support.

The first priority of India's foreign policy should be to consolidate and update its cooperative relations with the neighbours, not only in South Asia but also in Central, South East and West Asia. In all these regions, important changes are taking place, and that is where imaginative initiatives are called for.

On a bilateral basis, India has been able to impressively upgrade its relations with its South Asian neighbours. Though Indo-Pak relations still remain acrimonous, India's relations with Nepal, Bangladesh and Sri Lanka have taken a turn for the positive.

Credit for improvements in Indo-Nepal relations is largely due to the first democratic head of Nepal, Mr Bhattarai, who appreciated India's security sensitivities and saw the futility of acquiring mini-arms dumps when the world was moving in another direction and India, in no way, posed any threat to its neighbours.

With the transfer of the Teen Bigha, an outstanding issue was sorted with Bangladesh, our thanks are mainly due to the then Chief Minister of West Bengal, Mr Jyoti Basu.

Another neighbourhood of this subcontinent is Central Asia, where pronounced uncertainties prevail. Unfortunately, thanks to our legacy of the past, our diplomacy has not devoted the needed time and attention to this large and diverse region that extends from Mongolia and Kazakistan to trans Caucasia. There is a sudden explosion of unfamiliar ideas, alliances and conflicts. Almost every new state is embroiled in dispute with the neighbours or is busy writing secessionist eruptions. The idea of a Pan-Turkic block threatens territorial integrities of many countries ranging from the Arabic States to China.

Azarbaijan is an example worth studying to understand as to

115

what could happen elsewhere in Central Asia and Caucasia. Nationalist upsurges there poses very problematic implications. Ethnically Turkish, the Azarbaijanians do not accept the Iranian model of a fundamentalist state; while they prefer the Turkish secular model there is a movement to create a 'Greater Azarbaijan' by including 20 million Azeris living in North Iran.

Iran is countering the Armenian and Georgian States. The Azeris also fear that the USA at some stage might support Christian Armenia. Unless the Russian-led Commonwealth of Independent States (CIS) or Russia itself intervenes to end such mini wars, regional instability could flow out in several directions, including ours.

While talking of Central Asia, one cannot ignore the Uzbeki nationalism that is trying to have its way in Kirgzia. It has already fought a war with the Turks in Farghana and Tashkent. Conflict between various Turki sub-nationalities are destroying the pipe dream of a greater Turkistan.

These events in the Northern neighbourhood of the South Asian subcontinent have serious implications for other countries in this region particularly when new types of regional groupings are being hawked around.

During my tenure as Prime Minister, newly independent Central Asian States with the exception of Kazakistan that preferred an Observer status, joined ECO (Economic Cooperation Council) comprising Iran, Turkey and Pakistan. The ECO Summit promised to create a powerful Islamic Market and it hoped that Afghanistan and Bangladesh will soon join in.

Some scribes then spoke of a 'powerful Islamic state', wherein two of its members, Pakistan and Kazakistan have nuclear weapons and several others possess tactical nuclear weapons of the former Soviet State.

It would be erroneous to go by all that is being claimed. All former members of the Soviet state are very much linked with the CIS and the economy of the Russian state. Their adverse economic situations make them vulnerable. Besides, none of the non-CIS members of ECO enjoy such affluence as to under-write their needs for economic stablisation and development. Iran could help but only marginally.

Iran and Turkey have their own rivalling regional interests. Teheran spearheads a Caspian Sea Cooperation Zone to entice Russia, Kazakistan and Turkmenistan.

Turkey, on the other hand, is launching a rival Black Sea Cooperation Council comprising Turkey, Azerbiajan, Bulgaria, Rumania, Ukraine, Georgia, Moldovia and Russia.

Policy makers in Delhi have to keep in mind the future role of Russia in this region. The Communist regime of seventy years had succeeded in modernizing social outlooks and transformed institutions in the region. Even when religion comes back to them, hopefully, it will adopt a secular milieu.

While reacting to these happenings, India should keep in mind the fact that it enjoys high prestige in the region. Its rela-tionship with Russia will continue on a firm footing. It must be said to the credit of Indian diplomacy that it is not acting in haste nor trying to transplant the Indo-Pak acrimony in this area.

Indian Foreign Policy cannot be and is not a captive of situa-tions in the North. It has to pay due, and even slightly more than due, attention to the Indian Ocean Rim countries. That is where commonality of interest between India and Sri Lanka gets pro-nounced. In saying this I do not mean, in any way, to understate interests of Maldives, Bangladesh and Pakistan and also the two landlocked members of SAARC, Nepal and Myanmar.

In the Cold War era, all of us in the subcontinent along with several other nations in NAM had made gigantic but unsuccess-ful efforts to transform the Indian Ocean to a zone of peace. With the end of the Cold War, the superpower confrontation in these waters has ended. Then why these mounting expenses and ever increasing military presence?

As far as the countries of the Indian Ocean are concerned,

they may sometime clash with neighbours. But neither individually nor jointly can they pose any threat to the US.

Sustained, blocked and punitive actions against Iraq have unveiled a new US strategy. It is now evolving a security system in the North Western part of the Indian Ocean, by including the countries of the Gulf along with Syria and Egypt, to sign a treaty of some sort.

Exorcising the haunting ghost of Saddam Hussein is very handy for the US strategists who benefit a great deal from regional rivalries and faulty security doctrines that invite extra-territorial presence and interventions.

It is now clear, if there was any doubt, that a subtle US strategy first built Iraq's military machine and then destroyed it. A myopic Saddam facilitated this task. The war aims of UN Security Council and the USA did not coincide. The US was more keen to destroy Iraq and eliminate the emergence of any autonomous power in the Gulf.

The Secretary of State, Mr Baker (Jr) had reminded me in those tumultous days of the Gulf Crisis that sources of energy were of vital interest to their security and economy and the US would not permit anyone to control them exclusively.

In strategic terms, the Russian threat has disappeared and may not come back for quite some time. But the US now apprehends threat to her interests from the Third World countries, particularly those which are rushing to develop nuclear weapons. This fear has been aggravated by the prevailing turmoil in ex-Soviet States and efforts on the parts of Iran and Pakistan to lay their hands on available fission materials. Indian diplomacy had its own dilemmas regarding the NPT.

When we look at the contours of the Indo-US relations that are presently a primary focus of India's Foreign Policy, we will realize that complex strategic political and economic situations confront us.

Dissolution of the Soviet Union has placed the Indo-US

relationship in a new framework. In its contemporary phase, Washington's strategic needs and requirements in South Asia have undergone a change. It requires eclipsing the past to explore areas of fruitful cooperation. The White House has appreciated Indian concerns and policies regarding Kashmir.

It is an evidence of the changed times and relations that Washington appreciated India's policies during the Gulf crisis and did not press it to join the war even symbolically, despite the fact that Pakistan had lent its troops.

The two countries have stepped up interaction between their armed forces, building a cooperative and mutually-beneficial relationship.

Unilateral invocation of Super 301 and US reaction to the Indo-Russia Agreement for acquisition of cryogenic engines are two such examples that have caused deep concern to India. Research and Development of India's Space Programme occupies a position of importance in India's vision of future.

In the overall context, it is important for both India and US to sustain an upswing in bilateral relations. Both must continue to discover wider pastures of cooperation while avoiding to tread on each other's sensitivities.

This is a selective presentation of the issues and situations that face Indian diplomacy that is also, at the same time, confronted with militancies in some states that are aided and abetted from abroad, causing severe strains on foreign relationships.

I hope I have, to some extent, if not in full, been able to present a picture of the dilemmas and challenges that India's foreign Policy has been facing.

14

Essentials of International Economic Cooperation*

The beginning of the 1990s witnessed remarkable and unprecedented changes, some of which took place at a breathtaking pace. The East-West detente improved prospects for disarmament as well as for finding solutions to a large number of regional conflicts which had proved intractable until recently. With the improvement in the relationship between the big powers, UN was in a better position to play the role envisaged for it in the Charter to achieve peace, security and prosperity for all.

India rejoiced at the entry of Namibia into our family of independent nations. The raising of independent Namibia's flag was a proud moment not only for the valiant people of Namibia but for freedom-loving people everywhere. In congratulating our brethren in Namibia, we congratulated ourselves. I also congratulated the UN for its successful role in giving concrete shape to the cherished goal of the brave and courageous people of Namibia.

Eastern Europe has seen a movement in the direction of democracy, multi-party government, pluralism, exercise of basic human rights, the opening up of economies and their integration

---

*Statement delivered at the 18th special session of the UN General Assembly, New York on 23/4/1990.

with the world economy as a whole. Seldom in modern history have we seen such a decisive and powerful assertion of the people's will.

The formal closing of the Cold War and the erosion of the rivalry among hostile power blocs was a vindication of one of the principal objectives of the Non-Aligned Movement. As a democratic society wedded to a multi-party system and mixed economy, India welcomed the changes taking place in Eastern Europe. We have always had a deep and abiding commitment to individual rights and liberties and have always kept the upliftment of the common man as the central objective of our development process.

It was but natural for us to hope that these favourable developments would also lead to an improvement in the prospects of millions in the developing countries, still afflicted by abject poverty.

Unfortunately, positive developments on the political and security side were not matched by progress in the economic sphere for the developing countries. International economic co-operation, and particularly constructive dialogue needed to nurture it; this remained frozen. Meanwhile, the gap between the developed and developing countries widened even further. The developing countries as a whole felt excluded from the recent growth in the world economy. Even though some of them maintained a growth momentum, the vast majority of them were rendered worse off compared to what they were a decade ago.

Nowhere was this more starkly evident than in many countries of Africa and Latin America, for whom the 1980s was truly a 'lost decade'. Several developing countries, already at the margin of survival, experienced zero or negative growth rates during this period. The accumulated problems of human deprivation, crumbling infrastructure, environmental degradation and crushing indebtedness to the developing countries continue to be a challenge not only for the countries of Africa but for the entire

121

international community. Only a global effort can solve the pervasive crisis confronting the developing countries. Failure of such an effort would not only bring added misfortune to their suffering people but have far-reaching global consequences as well.

We feared that if the emerging economic compulsions were not adequately accommodated, the resulting strains could undermine the current trend towards global peace and harmony. A detente devoid of economic content was unlikely to endure.

The world economy continues to undergo radical changes. Rapid developments in science and technology have transformed the patterns of production, consumption and trade. The revolution in communication and information technologies has led to an unprecedented integration of the world economy and unification of capital and other markets. These developments, along with the growing understanding of environmental threats to the planet, have heightened the awareness of interdependence among nations and inter-relationship between issues. Today, the impact of events in one part of the globe is almost instantaneously felt in all other parts. The unprecedented dimensions and the pace of technological and financial change have added to the complexity of global economic problems and also led to the emergence of new problems, which can be solved only by nations acting together, and not each of them going its own way. The limitations of a unilateral or ad hoc approach have become all too obvious.

The time has now come to take stock of these developments and assess their implications for the growth and development of developing countries. Global peace and security have to be nurtured and underpinned by parallel and complementary efforts at reducing economic disparities and inequities. Durable peace cannot be built on the shifting sands of economic uncertainties.

Developing countries had little to rejoice in for what the 1980s bought them. It was during this period that we saw one of the worst anomalies of our time, i.e. the net transfer of resources from developing to developed countries. An increasing number of developing countries have fallen in the debt trap. This period has also seen the growing proliferation of protectionist measures, many of which were adopted by developed countries in a discriminatory manner against developing countries. The repeated commitments of these countries to adhere to a standstill on such measures had lost all credibility because of frequent departures from it. Commodity prices touched historically low levels. Financial and monetary imbalances in developed countries adversely affected the economies of developing countries through higher rates of interest, exchange rate fluctuations and general condition of uncertainty in the world of money and capital markets. Development assistance is fast losing its earlier pioneering role and is now tied to too many conditionalities and cross-conditionalities. Technology transfers continue to be obstructed by their prohibitive prices and numerous restrictive business practices. On top of all this, we have seen a growing tendency to bring in increasing number of emerging technologies under restrictive regimes which are designed to serve non-economic objectives.

Despite these impediments which are a legacy of the 1980s, most developing countries are experimenting with wide-ranging policy reforms, involving adoption of more open economic policies aimed at integrating their economies into the mainstream of the world economy. The European countries, too, are undertaking far-reaching economic restructuring. The entry of an increasing number of countries into the main-stream of global economy is a trend which is in the interest of all countries and ought to be encouraged. However, this process is bound to impose economic and financial constraints and even create social tensions and conflicts. This entails risks as well as opportunities. The success of these strategies requires a much more open and cooperative world economy, vastly expanded flow of concessional resources and renewed confidence of the developing countries

123

in the multilateral trading system. This alone can give the developing countries the degree of flexibility and confidence that is essential for taking this process to its logical conclusion.

The current detente is a window of opportunity for the international community. It is based on the realization of the impending danger to the survival of human species posed by the nuclear arms race, degradation of the environment and such other non-military threats to security as hunger, squalor, disease, illiteracy and gross economic inequality, both within and among nations. The solution to such vast and complex problems calls for a concerted and coherent approach within a multilateral framework.

The tasks facing us will become much easier if they are undertaken within the framework of an expanding and growing world economy. The major challenge lies in working out a package of measures which ensures the return of the world economy to a higher growth trajectory.

Growth in the world economy can prove to be lasting and self-sustaining only if all its constituent parts grow in harmony. The existence at the same time of under-utilized capacity and structural unemployment in developed countries and vast potential demand in developing countries, calls for a bolder initiative for substantial injection of purchasing power, particularly in the economies of the latter group of countries. This will not only accelerate development in developing countries but will also mitigate the imbalances in the world economy.

What is needed, first and foremost, is to reinstate the objective of development in the centre of international economic co-operation and bring the focus back to the crucial issues of poverty and underdevelopment. Unfortunately, this perspective has for some time been overshadowed by preoccupation with short-term measures of adjustment. Issues of reform and adjustment can be seen in all their implications and tackled most effectively only if they are firmly put in the development context.

124

Accelerating development requires, above all, a substantial increase in the net transfer of concessional resources for revitalizing the development process in the developing countries and liberating them from the shackles of external debt. To this end, the resource base of international financial institutions requires to be considerably expanded so that they can retain the flexibility needed to respond to different situations prevailing in different groups of developing countries. The events of the recent past, particularly the emergence of debt crisis, have shown that commercial flows are no substitute for multilateral flows. Expanded multilateral lending is vital for accelerating development. What is needed is not only the management and eventual liquidation of the existing debt problems of developing countries; equally significant is the adoption of anticipatory measures, such as increased concessional financing, designed to prevent the emergence of debt crises in countries which have so far avoided the debt trap. Suitable mechanisms should be devised to mobilise surplus resources of developed countries to meet the needs of development finance for developing countries.

With the commencement of the process of nuclear disarmament and vastly improved prospects for conventional disarmament in Europe, there is now a real opportunity of additional resources being released in sizable quantity from the military sector, being available for developmental purposes. The cost of disarmament measures is often exaggerated. It is not even a fraction of the disarmament dividend and the bulk of it is of a one-time nature. On the other hand, the size of the disarmament dividend was a reality, which was borne out by the fact that the Pentagon had prepared a phased programme of reduction in the US defence budget to almost half its size, that the Soviet Union had started adopting conversion measures and that countries which were in the past not prepared to get involved in any discussion on conversion agreed to go this far, amounts to a great achievement by the United Nations. The size of the disar-

125

mament dividend can be tremendously enlarged and social and economic difficulties that arise in the initial phase, can be greatly minimised if the process of conversion is planned in advance.

We recognize that the internal demands of the major military spenders will inevitably be the first claimants of the peace dividend. Far from being concerned by it, we regard this as a welcome development as it would have a salutary effect on the world economy. Our first priority should be to insulate the world economy from the distortions which excessive military expenditure inevitably causes. This will be to the benefit of all. At the same time, we should take advantage of the favourable situation to make appropriate institutional arrangements within the United Nations, for giving concrete shape to the idea of a link between disarmament and development which has been accepted in principle by the international community.

Multilateral institutions designed to promote economic cooperation should be strengthened and made effective. The present asymmetrical treatment of the developing countries in these institutions should be redressed. The norms, rules and regulations underpinning these institutions should be fair and equitable and should be scrupulously observed. Whenever necessary, they should be updated and revamped, taking into account the current reality. It is essential to restore to the international monetary system its essential underpinning to exchange rate stability and adequate official liquidity.

India has a vital stake in an open and liberal trading system within the framework of GATT and regarded the Uruguay Round of Multilateral Trade Negotiations as of critical importance in this context. We participated in these negotiations in good faith and in pursuit of the common objective of preserving and strengthening the multilateral trading system.

The declaration launching these negotiations in Punta del Este, clearly recognizes that the purpose of the Uruguay Round was not only to liberalize trade but also to keep in mind the

126

developmental needs of developing countries. Liberalization was not considered as an end in itself but as a means to meet the development needs of developing countries. It was also agreed that areas of concern of developing countries would be accorded high priority in the process of the negotiations and that these countries would not be expected to make concessions which are inconsistent with their development needs.

Unfortunately, we witnessed a growing imbalance developing in these negotiations. Issues of great concern to developing countries, such as textiles, tropical products and non-discriminatory safeguards were being pushed to the back burner and greater importance was attached to the new areas which were primarily of interest to developed countries. For achieving the objective of the Uruguay Round, it was essential that the outcome be balanced and issues of interest to developing countries effectively addressed. It is also important to realize that there are obvious limitations, imposed by their technological and developmental requirements and by the need to serve the public interest, on the capacity of developing countries to liberalise in the new areas.

There is also an incipient danger of the regionalization and vivisection of world trade. It is vitally important that regional trade groupings among developed countries emerging in different parts of the world, do not acquire a discriminatory character and become 'fortresses' to those falling outside these groupings. Going by past experience, the fear that these groupings might turn protectionist is not totally unfounded. In any case, it devolves on these groupings to take concerete measures to demonstrate this fear to be untrue.

The management of the world economy needs to be more broad-based so as to reflect the interests of all countries and groups of countries, and to evolve policies which can be supported and implemented by all. The current economic and social problems and the needs of the future are such that no single nation or group of nations can solve them in isolation. They call for a joint effort based on mutuality of interest.

The degradation of the environment poses a threat to human survival. This calls for urgent cooperative measures for ensuring environmentally sustainable developments. In this, the prevailing asymmetry in the level of production and consumption in developed and developing countries should be fully taken into account. No attempt should be made to find solutions based on a freezing of the level and pattern of development in developing countries.

Through the best part of the 1980s, there was a retreat from, and a concerted attack on, multilateralism. In this process, the role of the United Nations, in undertaking negotiations on economic issues of vital concern to humankind, got seriously undermined. Even though in the context of the new detente, the UN's role in the political and security sector has been revived, major developed countries showed no disposition to entrust to the United Nations its legitimate responsibility in the economic field. The United Nations is the only international organization with universal membership mandated by its Charter to discharge responsibilities for promoting development. It is, therefore, essential to put the development issues back on the agenda of the United Nations.

India sees this as an opportunity to broaden international understanding and strengthen multilateral cooperation in the economic sphere in full consciousness that peace itself will be endangered unless growing disparities are redressed. In this increasingly complex and interdependent world, vastly enhanced international economic cooperation has become an absolute imperative. We must therefore, resolve to break out of the present no-growth and low-growth syndrome and aim at qualitatively higher levels of growth for all the constituent parts of the world economy. This alone will enable us to make a concerted attack on poverty and underdevelopment and come to grips with

128

numerous social and infrastructural problems clamouring for attention even in developed countries.

We must commit ourselves to take all measures needed to accomplish this noble task and bring the multilateral institutions under the aegis of the United Nations—our instrument for achieving this goal.

15

The End of the Cold War

India was one of the relatively small number of states that were present at the creation of the United Nations. The UN was born of a war-shattered world's hope that it would be the benign, sometime stern, guardian of a world, committed to peace and cooperation among nations. Unfortunately, the end of the Second World War did not bring peace; it brought a long, often icy, Cold War. Scores of new nations in Asia and Africa emerged as sovereign states from the crumbling empires of Europe. The Cold War had a negative impact on the life of these new nations. We in the so-called Third world remained firmly committed to the United Nations as the only organization that could usher in world peace and promote global well-being. The vicissitudes through which the UN passed did not diminish our faith in this august body.

We, the nations of the South, had special reason to rejoice at the end of the Cold War. India was all the more happy because from the very moment of its Independence, it sought the termination of this power struggle. We joined other nations to enunciate the principle of Non-Alignment to protect the independence of the new nations and their right to choose for themselves the kind of international relations they wished to have and the models of development they wished to adopt. We welcomed the collapse of the Cold War divide. The Cold War mindset, which took deep roots in our minds, would yield to a new mindset of global detente and cooperation.

An event of special importance in this context was the German unification. This reflected the fulfilment of the deepest aspirations of the German people. In the new Europe which was emerging, a united Germany—in the model foreseen by a great son of Germany, Thomas Mann—would be a powerful factor in favour of stability and peaceful cooperation. India looked forward to working closely with united Germany in the cause of peace and progress around the world.

India has always rejected the logic of the Cold War and the division of the international community into opposing blocs. In accordance with our policy of non-alignment, we sought to simultaneously build relations of trust and friendship with both the Soviet Union and the United States. The replacement of East-West confrontation by a new cooperative approach greatly facilitated our task. The year 1989 saw a further strengthening of our ties with the great democracy of the United States. With our time-tested friend, the Soviet Union, we added new dimensions to our friendly cooperation. We hailed the historic endeavours of the Soviet people to reshape their political and economic structures on the basis of democracy, unity and economic efficiency.

The United Nations was a participant in many of the momentous changes during the year. Its work in Namibia and Nicaragua provided splendid examples of its role, testifying to its renewed relevance and effectiveness in international affairs. And a great deal of the credit should go to the then UN Secretary General, Mr Perez de Cuellar, for his patient, prudent, painstaking and imaginative management of the world body.

The Secretary General perceptively observed in his 1990 Report to the organization that:

131

It has been a wholesome development of recent years that the international discourse has been disburdened of excessive ideological or rhetorical baggage. It is far easier to accommodate contentious interests or claims, honestly stated, than to reconcile opposing doctrines. If the new mood of pragmatism which has released us from the thraldom of the Cold War is to spread all over the world, nations need to shed the vestigial prejudices of former times and couch their dialogue in terms of common sense and plain justice.

These are truly wise words spoken at a critical turn of history. India was always among the many nations who wished to see the United Nations emerge as the pivot and fulcrum of international peace and security. The new effectiveness of the United Nations owed a great deal to the fact that the earlier confrontational relationship between the great powers gave way to a detente which, in turn, led to a new collaborative relationship. A cooperative relationship among the major powers is a necessary, but not a sufficient, condition for true multilateralism. The latter requires full and equal participation of all nations—big and small—in the multilateral decision-making process. The great issues of the day can no longer be decided in the capitals of a few major powers.

The voice of the majority must not only be heard but also respected. The democratic principle is an essential requirement of a genuinely multilateral system. Nor can the concerns of the deprived majority of the world's population be denied priority on the international agenda. Peace and development are closely interrelated and deserve equal attention. In the final analysis, the success of the United Nations will be measured in terms of its ability to reflect and meet the concerns of the majority of humankind.

India was gravely concerned at the crisis in the Gulf. India's position was, and remained, clear and consistent. We were

132

against the use or threat of force in the settlement of differences in inter-state relations. We firmly opposed aggression. The crisis had arisen from the Iraqi invasion of Kuwait. It followed that Iraq must withdraw its forces from Kuwait, as demanded by the Security Council. India did not recognize Kuwait's annexation. India fully subscribed to and strictly abided by all the resolutions of the Security Council concerning this crisis. The crisis led to the induction of foreign forces into the Gulf region. In the changed world environment, permanent foreign military presence was not desired by any country, nor was it in anyone's interest.

Since ages India maintained the most cordial and friendly relations with Kuwait and Iraq. Almost 2,00,000 of our nationals, who were present in these countries when the crisis erupted, found themselves caught up in its coils. Provision of essential food supplies for them, and other innocent victims from Third World countries, was a matter of the highest importance, from the humanitarian point of view, to the entire world community.

In West Asia, there can be no durable peace without a just and comprehensive settlement based on the inalienable rights of the Palestinian people to self-determination, as well as the right of all states in the region, including Palestine and Israel, to live in peace and security within internationally recognized borders, in accordance with UN Security Council Resolutions 242 and 338. Israel's attempts to suppress the *Intifadah* or to block progress towards a dialogue could not succeed.

India reaffirmed its solidarity with the people of Cyprus, which partly remained under foreign occupation. We fully supported the sovereignty, unity and territorial integrity of that country.

Some of the most hopeful developments during the year were related to Southern Africa. We warmly welcomed independent Namibia into the community of nations. Developments in South Africa held promise of real progress.

Nelson Mandela, freed after spending a quarter of a century

behind bars, galvanized the currents of peaceful change. We welcomed the talks initiated between the African National Conference (ANC) and the South African Government to clear the way for negotiations on a new non-racial constitution.

While racism was on the retreat in South Africa, in Fiji, a constitution had been imposed which institutionalized racial discrimination. The Suva regime flouted internationally accepted principles of democracy and human rights. Its undemocratic and racially discriminatory policies were unacceptable.

In the Korean peninsula, there were some encouraging signs of reconciliation and dialogue. We regarded the historic meetings between the Prime Ministers of the Democratic People's Republic of Korea and the Republic of Korea as a major step forward. We supported all efforts aimed at the peaceful reunification of these two nations. And in conformity with the principle of universality, we further supported the aspirations of the Korean people to be represented in the United Nations, so that they could actively contribute towards the realisation of the purposes and principles of the UN.

There had been encouraging progress towards a resolution of the Cambodian problem. The Djakarta Meeting and the decision of the Supreme National Council held the promise of an early return to normalcy. We hoped that a settlement of the problem would fully reflect Cambodia's sovereignty and independence and ensure that its people could exercise their democratic rights to determine their own destiny free from foreign interference and intervention.

Myanmar continued to be held in thrall by forces unwilling to accept the decision that its people took in the national elections. We called upon Yangon to accept the people's verdict and work with the latter to establish peace and democracy in the country.

Relations with our northern neighbour, People's Republic of China, showed steady and welcome improvement. Both countries have expressed their determination to settle the boundary question through peaceful and friendly consultations and also to develop relations actively in a variety of other fields.

We believed that full and faithful implementation of the Geneva Agreements, so arduously architectured by the Secretary General of the UN, would restore normalcy, stabilize the life and security of the Afghan people and also help in furthering the cause of peace and good neighbourliness in South Asia.

We warmly welcomed the return of democracy in neighbouring Nepal. Differences which had earlier crept into our relations were happily and speedily resolved after the transition in Nepal thus reflecting the deep aspirations for peace shared by the two neighbours.

Pakistan has been nursing and arming terrorist activities in Jammu and Kashmir, causing immense human suffering, extensive misery and loss of innocent lives. All efforts on our part to persuade the Government of Pakistan to desist from these activities were first ignored and then rejected. Characteristically, Pakistan denied responsibility and involvement in these acts. The Indo-Pak Simla Agreement, signed in 1972, fully spelt out these principles and despite Pakistan's blatant violation, India continued its quest to consolidate a relationship of cordiality and friendship between the people of the two countries.

Arms race, support to terrorism and aggressive polemics only add to tensions and create a climate of instability—which is so much out of place in the contemporary global environment. We proposed to Pakistan a set of measures that would induce mutual confidence and cooperation. But unfortunately, Pakistan chose to ignore them and to persist in its unacceptable activities.

India and Pakistan can have a great future if we respect each other's integrity and unity, and if Pakistan desists from the temptation of interfering in our internal affairs. It is in this spirit that I will not refer to the gross flouting of human rights in Pakistan, particularly in Sind and Baluchistan.

135

We believed that regional organizations had acquired an added relevance and could play an important role in promoting international cooperation. In our region, SAARC was making a most valuable contribution by fostering a climate of constructive cooperation. We looked forward to a steady expansion of its activities and hoped that Afghanistan and a democratic Myanmar would join this organization to build an era so needed in our part of the world.

The reordering of Eastern Europe was epoch-making. India welcomed this reaffirmation of the democratic spirit. The changes in this region had understandably prompted the generous instincts of the industrialised world. We hoped that Eastern Europe's integration into the world economy would serve the interests of all nations. We looked forward to strengthening our ties of cooperation with these countries. At the same time, we also expected that the East-West thaw should not result in depriving the developing world of increased economic assistance.

The end of the Cold War, we felt, was the most opportune time for the international community to question the validity of theories that sought to justify continuation of nuclear weapons. Inter-state relations should be based on cooperation and dialogue instead of mutual fears and frozen hostility. A new international security order needs to be created to prepare us to move towards a nuclear weapon-free world. The action plan put forward by India for a nuclear weapon-free and non-violent world order outlined a systematic, rational and practicable time-frame to achieve these objectives.

The positive development during the years since the UN Conference on Disarmament and Development only further vindicated the essential premises of that Conference. We were seriously exploring the actual ways and means of channelling the peace dividend for the development of the countries of the South which had to face the adverse economic consequences of the unprecedented arms build-up of the past decade.

Economic growth had shown a mixed record. Expansion of world trade and output had begun to slow down. External and fiscal imbalances among the major economies persisted, aggravating the uncertainties facing developing countries. Monetary instability and higher interest rates added to their formidable economic problems. The international economic environment was inhospitable, as protectionism and discriminatory trade practices, inadequate financial flows, low commodity prices and exclusion from international economic decision-making process all conspired to make developing countries insecure and vulnerable. The Iraq-Kuwait crisis worsened this enfeeblement by raising oil prices, interrupting oil supplies and, in general, handicapping growth efforts.

While new problems arose, long-standing ones like external debt constrained development prospects. Some welcome initiatives were taken but proved inadequate to deal with the magnitude of the problem. Difficulties of many countries were overlooked, pointing to the inescapable need for a comprehensive and durable solution to the debt problem. Such a solution had to include anticipatory measures to prevent further proliferation of the debt problem to countries which despite serious difficulties were continuing to service their debts.

An International Development Strategy for the 1990s was being formulated. Its agenda was to determine whether the world carried over into the twenty-first century, the present legacy of poverty, underdevelopment and stagnation or whether it embarked on a more productive era, aiming at qualitatively higher levels of human welfare, affording all countries and all peoples an equitable opportunity to prosper in a stable and predictable external environment. This guiding principle of international cooperation underlined our efforts in all the sectoral areas of the strategy. We hoped that we would quickly be able to conclude negotiations, so that the international community had before it a coherent and identifiable framework of goals and objectives

137

and a consistent set of policy measures to which all countries stood committed.

The North-South dialogue, once nurtured by the international community, had fallen into neglect. It deserved to be revived. When political cooperation was on the upswing, why should economic cooperation languish? The head and the limbs had to function together if the body was to be strong. India has traditionally had the privilege, in this context, of working with other countries to make a North-South compact real and forceful.

The South-South cooperation to build up collective self-reliance was an important aspect of international economic growth. The Summit in Kuala Lumpur of fifteen developing countries including India provided a significant impetus to this process.

We were also awaiting the conclusion of the Uruguay Round. A great deal of expectation had been aroused in these negotiations and we were participating with the hope that the conclusions of the Uruguay Round would assist developing countries. Despite very severe economic difficulties, many developing countries including India made offers to their utmost ability. These were, however, not reciprocated, particularly in areas to which developing countries have attached importance such as textile, agriculture, tropical products and safeguards. It was difficult to visualize a balanced outcome of the Uruguay Round without substantial progress in these and other areas of greatest concern to developing countries.

Environmental concerns rightly moved to a top position in the international agenda. The UN Conference on Environment focused on the inescapable fact that protection of the environment required acceleration of development in the poorer countries.

At the heart of the environmental crisis lay the persistence of wide disparities in levels of production and consumption between the developed and the developing countries. The very high per capita consumption levels in the industrialized world imposed corresponding strain on global natural resources and thus on the environment. On the other hand, extreme poverty in the developing countries was itself a cause of environmental degradation. In order to simply survive, poverty-stricken people were forced, for example, to cut down forests for firewood or overgraze pastures. The environment could not be protected in the developing countries unless the root cause of its degradation, namely poverty, was eradicated. Thus, sustainable development called for curbs on extravagant lifestyles in affluent countries and promotion of economic development in less fortunate areas. Sustainable development can only be equitable development. The call for a change in life-styles in affluent societies does not imply a reduction in living standards; indeed, it envisages an improvement in the overall quality of life.

It is now accepted that environmental protection required the provision of new and additional funds for developing countries as well as the transfer of an environmentally benign technology to these countries on a preferential basis. Any new environmental regulatory mechanisms should be accompanied from the outset by full and adequate provision for funding the technology transfer. This is an essential requirement for effective action on the environment.

In conclusion, 1990 marked the end of a long historical period and cross over to another epoch. We now have to put our heads and hearts together to design a world of peace and development. We have to fashion the United Nations to reflect the end of the Cold War, making it responsive to the diversity of the world community, and representative of world democracy and equality of sovereign nations. Let the new era usher in world peace and a global fabric of cooperation. Let us all work together towards that noble objective.

16

CTBT and India's Security

WE PRESERVE THE SOVEREIGN RIGHT TO SECURITY
—*The Telegraph:* 28 June 1996

The new External Affairs Minister, Mr Inder Kumar Gujral, is an old hand at his job, having been one of the country's senior most diplomats. He has moved into his job with relative ease. Indian Foreign Service officials are comfortable working with him, as he knows most of them from his earlier stint. Mr Gujral spoke to *The Telegraph* on a number of issues, expressing India's concerns and the task before the new government to improve relations with neighbours.

Q: Now that India has decided not to sign the Comprehensive Test Ban Treaty (CTBT), what will be the next step?
A: As far as we are concerned, negotiations are continuing in Geneva. We have made our position clear, having done so, we are watching how the world powers react. That is why our Ambassador continues to participate in the discussions.

Q: The US thinks India might still change its mind on CTBT.
A: Let us see, generalized statements do not mean much. Naturally we will respond to the situation as it develops. This is why we have not walked out. As a matter of tradition, Indian diplo-

macy has never walked out of any international forum. We have never slammed the door on negotiations. We feel that in the context of the post-Cold War era, particularly, talks must never be closed.

Q: India has been insisting on a provision for a timeframe. Does it mean that we stick to our position if it is not included, or is there chance of compromise?
A: Timeframe is not an abstract formulation. The pertinent point is to ask ourselves, does the world feel comfortable with a mounting heap of nuclear arms and their additional sophistication? Therefore when we refer to a timeframe, we want people to understand whether the future of the world is dismal or hopeful.

Q: India has not carried out a nuclear test since 1974. What does it mean when you talk about India keeping its nuclear options open?
A: It means that we do not decide our arms policy in the abstract. What type of defence preparation India should have is born out of security perceptions and the threat perceptions at a particular time. So when we talk of keeping our nuclear options, it means we preserve the sovereign right of the country to look after its security.

Q: Do we expect pressure from any quarter for our present stand?
A: There is only one pressure and that is my commitment to my country. It is our responsibility to see that India's security is adequately cared for. The foremost responsibility of any government is to see that under all circumstances, the security and defence of the country are not compromised.

Q: Will the thrust of your foreign policy be on improving India's relations with its neighbours?
A: That is, of course, the tradition of India. We do care more for

our relations with our neighbours. It has acquired added importance since the end of the Cold War. What is called globalization, in reality, means that regional cooperation has come to the fore, whether you think in terms of European Union, or the ASEAN. When we talk of cooperation in terms of our neighbours in the SAARC, we try to keep in step with the world.

Q: You also talk of expanding SAARC membership.
A: What I mean is that our SAARC partners might consider the option of including Myanmar and Afghanistan and build cooperative relations with Central Asian nations. This would enlarge the economic potential and very soon become an important market in the world.

Q: You have spoken of adopting the Indo-China model in improving relations with Pakistan. But with Islamabad's insistence on solving the Kashmir issue first, do you think this will work?
A: We are talking in terms of reality. The Prime Minister of Pakistan has written to our Prime Minister and me, to which we have responded. We have made our intentions known.

Q: How are our relations with the US?
A: One point must be kept in mind that our relationship with the US was always multi-dimensional. When I look at overall relations with the US, it gives me satisfaction and happiness. We cooperate in several international fora. It will be a mistake to believe that if we differ on some issues, it will sour our relations.

Q: Will the stand taken by India on the CTBT not strain our ties with the US?
A: What we have said on CTBT is in context of our national security. That is how we look at it and I think every friendly country should appreciate this.

INDIA HAS NO FEAR OF ISOLATION: GUJRAL
—*The Economic Times:* 5 July 1996

External Affairs Minister I.K. Gujral says India does not fear global isolation on the nuclear test ban issue and is not prepared to 'climb down' from the stand that it has taken on the Comprehensive Test Ban Treaty (CTBT).

'National security interests are not safeguarded on the basis of votes taken or on the basis of how many supporters we have or how many we don't have,' Mr Gujral said, adding, 'no country in the world does it'.

'If there are some powers that think that they cannot go with us, I have nothing against them. But I would say: India cannot compromise its own security interests,' he said.

Asked if India was prepared to climb down for the sake of a compromise on the stalled treaty, Mr Gujral shot back: 'On security issues, how does one climb down?

'We are saying, please promise at least, even if you don't implement, that you are one day going to abolish all nuclear weapons. We are also saying, please take into account the security environment around India,' Mr Gujral said.

He said India will not react after assessing the reaction from world capitals as to whether Indian interests have been accommodated or not, but security will remain the 'bottom line and the front line' in any negotiation.

Mr Gujral, who has come back to steer Indian diplomacy after a gap of six years, said the CTBT issues apart, the 'central point of our foreign policy has to be to renew friendship and cooperation with our neighbours'.

He said India had responded 'positively' to the Pakistani leadership's overtures soon after Prime Minister HD Deve Gowda's government took over and was awaiting its response.

He said India had not reacted even when it was noticed that some public speeches of the Pakistani Prime Minister and Foreign Minister were not in the same spirit as the letters, 'because we do not want the process or the possibility of our dialogue to get thwarted in any way'.

He said 'India had, in fact, taken some "unilateral steps" to encourage people-to-people contact because the basic posture of Indian foreign policy is that we want to have friendly relations'.

Asked if India would respond to Pakistan's demands on what it calls the 'core issue' of Kashmir, Mr Gujral said he would not like to prejudge or prejudice the discussions, but would reiterate that India was 'prepared to discuss all subjects without preconditions on either side'.

To reports about a Sri Lankan offer of mediation at the instance of Pakistan, Mr Gujral said there was no such proposal from Sri Lankan Foreign Minister Lakshman Kadirgamar when he came recently and Colombo appreciates the fact that 'it is the bilateral dialogue that we are trying to activate between us and Pakistan'.

He said India would build very friendly relations with the United States. 'There are some issues on which we do not agree. But there are several issues on which we agree. And I emphasize more the areas where we agree than the areas where we do not agree,' Mr Gujral said.

He said he had not yet planned any visit to Washington but would visit New York in September to attend the UN General Assembly session.

INDIA WILL LOOK AFTER ITS OWN SECURITY
—Sunday: 7-13 July 1996

Mr Gujral is representative of a government which is made up of more than 20 different political parties. And with someone like Mulayam Singh Yadav making controversial statements—the last two were that India, Pakistan and Bangladesh should become a federation and that Pakistanis and Bangladeshis should be allowed to travel freely here—Mr Gujral has his job cut out for him.

Gujral has had a long diplomatic career. After a public spat with Sanjay Gandhi over a pro-Emergency broadcast over All India Radio, Gujral took up assignment as India's Ambassador to the Soviet Union at the height of the Cold War. At that time, world opinion was against Indira Gandhi's Emergency regime and it says something about Gujral's survivability that he remained at that job even after the Janata government came to power.

The Soviet experience gave him a sense of realpolitik. And being a Punjabi, he also has a special feeling for the Pakistani establishment and there was a little of the personal element in it when its Foreign Minister, Aseef Ahmad Ali praised Gujral as soon as he took over.

But he is still very pragmatic. Speaking to *Sunday*, Inder Kumar Gujral seemed undaunted by all this. Quietly forceful and completely comfortable with his assignment, he fielded a wide range of questions. Excerpts from the interview:

Sunday: The first Janata government's relations with Pakistan were better than the second Janata regime's, Why?
I.K. Gujral: Pakistan's interference in India's internal affairs increased particularly in 1989. Prime Ministers in the past have tried their best to improve relations. We in India, irrespective of the government in office, have tried to keep the relations warm and cordial with the Pakistani people and the government.

The Prime Minister and I have responded to their letters (showing interest in bilateral talks to resolve problems). We await their response.

Q: Does that also indicate greater trade between the two countries?

145

A: The South Asian Association for Regional Cooperation (SAARC) countries got together to introduce the era of South Asian Preferential Trade Agreement (SAPTA). The trade agreement has to be approved and permitted by SAARC laws. India has already endorsed it and now it is for Pakistan to decide. That will surely widen the area of trade between the two countries.

Q: Why didn't you sign the Comprehensive Test Ban Treaty (CTBT)?

A: India's policy ever since (Jawaharlal) Nehru's time has been in favour of nuclear disarmament. We have consistently been projecting the idea of not only a test ban but a ban on all weapons of mass destruction. And the CTBT was initially meant to do that but now we feel that the draft does not help fulfil the purpose.

The five nuclear powers have not promised to ban the weapons of mass destruction. Thus for me to be associated with something that is a mere charade is out of the question. Those who have the arms are trying to sermonise those who do not have arms. The draft treaty does not take care of all these things.

Q: What could be the consequences of all this?

A: The consequences can't be any because we are not the ones who have the arms. Relations between two in any case are not unilinear but multi-dimensional and they will continue to prosper.

Q: On the one hand China is supplying M-11s to Pakistan and on the other, we want to have a good relationship with China. Don't you see a contradiction there?

A: That is a question that should be answered by all those who have signed the Non-Proliferation Treaty (NPT). The NPT norms are being flouted time and again. India will look after its own

146

security. We have to periodically assess the threats and respond to them.

Q: Is there any need for India to declare itself as a nuclear power?
A: We have to settle everything according to our threat perceptions. When we say we preserve our options, it means we will respond to a situation as it develops. This is the ingredient of every country's foreign policy.

Q: What is the current position on India's efforts to become a member of the UN Security Council?
A: India is a contender for the South Asian seat. But Japan is also contending for that seat and that does not make sense. Japan should be considered for the Far Eastern seat.

Q: What is your position on the Burmese pro-democracy movement?
A: As a democracy we naturally have sympathy with all democracies. However, we do not believe in intervening from outside. We have sympathy with Myanmar as a country and hope that their problems will be sorted out democratically and peacefully. We are also keen on Myanmar becoming a part of SAARC, which can happen with the help of all SAARC nations.

Q: What is your view of the Tamil ethnic problem in Sri Lanka?
A: We respect the policies of President Chandrika Kumaratunga and have full faith in them. So far, she has been successful in sorting out the Tamil problems in Sri Lanka. We would definitely not like to interfere in their affairs. I only hope that the refugees can go back home with dignity and honour.

Q: Do you consider the infiltration of Bangladeshis into India to be as big a problem as the Bharatiya Janata Party (BJP) says it is?

A: Bangladesh has a new government. We would like to sort out all the existing problems with them.

Q: Do you intend to replace certain Ambassadors? Naresh Chandra, the Indian Ambassador to the US, was currently in the news.
A: I need not clarify that since there was no proposal to call Naresh Chandra back, postings will take place in the normal course.

IN OUR NATIONAL INTERESTS
—*Frontline:* 12 July 1986

External Affairs Minister, Inder Kumar Gujral is one of the most experienced members of the United Front Cabinet. Besides holding important portfolios including External Affairs in past Ministries, the suave politician was India's Ambassador to the Soviet Union in the late 1970s. He spoke to John Cherian in New Delhi on a wide range of issues on 22 June, soon after India's decision on the CTBT. Excerpts:

Q: What are your comments on the reaction to India's decision not to sign the CTBT?
A: The reactions of some countries are on expected lines. The decision taken by India is in conformity with our national interests. That is where the line is drawn. All the same, we have never slammed the door. We will continue to participate in discussions relating to various dimensions of the issue. In Indian diplomacy we have never walked out or slammed the door.

Q: Is there scope for improvement in bilateral links with Pakistan?
A: We have welcomed the two letters, one from the Pakistan Prime Minister and the other from the Foreign Minister, as soon

148

as our Prime Minister took office. We have responded to that with equal enthusiasm. We all feel that dialogue should continue so that it will lead to an environment of good neighbourliness. As we have said in our letter, we are prepared to discuss every issue without any preconditions on either side. Naturally the dialogue will have to begin at the level of officials but we will respond when we get an answer from the leadership of Pakistan to the Indian Prime Minister's letter.

Q: Is the focus of the new Government also going to be on economic diplomacy?
A: Economic diplomacy has come to occupy centrestage in the post-Cold War era the world over. That is the Indian perception too. Therefore we would like to cooperate with our near and distant neighbours to strengthen the Indian economy.

Q: What will be the foreign policy priorities?
A: We attach a great deal of importance to relations with neighbouring countries and also countries outside the region. For instance, India has become a dialogue partner with ASEAN (Association of South East Asian Nations). We have good relations with Central Asia and all the former Soviet states in the region. We would like to build on that. Our relations with the United States have been very cordial, of course; it has been our largest trade and economic partner. Sometimes there are different points of view but it goes to the credit of both countries that we have been able to work out amicable solutions. This will continue to be our approach. But we expect the United States to appreciate some of India's sensitivities.

Q: What about relations with Moscow?
A: Our relations with Russia have a long history which is very positive. Unfortunately, Russia had been going through a difficult phase but now its economy is slowly coming back to its

149

original shape. There is hardly an area, be it cultural, political or economic, in which we have not been close.

Q: Has Sri Lanka expressed any misgivings about the composition of the Government? There have been some reports in the Indian media.

A: The coming of the Sri Lankan Foreign Minister as our first guest after the formation of the new Government was very much appreciated. We consider this as a gesture of great friendship. We had an exchange of views in an atmosphere of cordiality and friendship. We expressed the hope that the situation in their country will improve to such an extent that they would be able to repatriate the several thousand displaced Sri Lankan refugees in Tamil Nadu and elsewhere. We want people to go back of their own free will. Nor will we exert any pressure on the displaced persons. India has promised to give a helping hand to Sri Lanka for the rehabilitation of the displaced persons.

Q: In recent times the tendency of Washington to impose unilateral economic blockades and trade embargoes on countries it does not like is causing great concern to the international community. What are your Government's views on the issue?

A: As a matter of policy we are against blockades and economic sanctions by one country against another. International cooperation suffers because of such policies. We hope that differences will be sorted out through dialogue and discussions. No one country should assume that it has the policing responsibilities.

THE RIGHT TO TEST
—Outlook: 17 July 1996

Foreign Minister I.K. Gujral spoke to Sunil Narula on India's retaining of the Nuclear option due to national security reasons and the country's threat perceptions. Excerpts:

India has always taken a moralistic stand on Nuclear disarmament. Why are we talking national security now?
I don't think we've ever taken any stand which didn't have the input of national security. It so happens that our national security and our moral posture coincided. Even today every country would be safe, including us, if there were no nuclear arms around. That's our general approach, and we continue to have it. In Geneva, we said that the treaty being drafted doesn't rid the world of nuclear arms. So when we say we are talking about security, it's not something new. Every country gives priority to its own security interests.

We never said it in so many words ...
I don't think so. Till now we'd been faced with one reality, that was the Cold War. Therefore, the articulation and the phraseology was different, our rhetoric was different. This conference is in a way a continuation of the NPT. Our policy regarding the NPT and this is consistent. We did not sign the NPT, we're not signing this. There is a clear linkage between our policy on the two.

In March, Salman Haider had said nuclear arms are not essential for our security. Isn't this contradictory?
When he said nuclear arms are not necessary for the world, he meant for everybody. He didn't mean everybody can have nuclear arms and India can feel secure. His statement has not been correctly understood.

What use is it to have an open nuclear option if we don't exercise it?
I've never said we won't exercise it. The question invariably asked is when? Now the 'when' is correlated with our assessment of threat. Whether it's a nuclear weapon or not, the weaponry is selected on the basis of threat perception. When we say our options are open, it means we'll act as per our threat perception.

151

It's thought if India conducts tests, the West will come down hard on us.

I'm not saying the world will come down hard on us or not, nor am I saying we should test or not. What I'm saying is, if at any stage our security planners come to the conclusion, which they have not now, that a test is called for, then whatever the world might say we may have to do it. Security decisions are not taken on the basis of referendum or popularity.

There's no transparency in our security policy.

Security policies are never transparent anywhere in the world. Do we know the security policy of all our neighbours? Do we know the weaponry they have?

India won't suffer if the Indian public is aware?

I'm all for open debate, but that doesn't mean you tell everyone, "I've got a knife in my pocket to defend myself".

Do we expect sanctions?

The issue is not sanctions. The point is, we've made it very clear that we're unable to sign the treaty as it is now drafted. We're meeting after a month, let's see if there's any change... if so, we'll act accordingly.

WHY INDIA DOES NOT SIGN THE TEST BAN TREATY
—International Herald Tribune: 26 August 1996

India has been widely criticized for blocking a nuclear test ban treaty that has taken more than two years to negotiate. On a visit to Singapore, Inder Kumar Gujral, the Indian Foreign Minister, discussed the issue with Michael Richardson of the International Herald Tribune.

Q: Why is India so strongly opposed to the proposed global treaty prohibiting nuclear tests?

A: Primarily because it fails to respond to the mandate given to it by the United Nations. That mandate said, in essence, that efforts should be made to free the world of nuclear weapons.

The five nuclear powers—the United States, China, Russia, France and Britain—have turned it around. They are trying to ban only nuclear weapon blasts. At the same time, they reserve for themselves the right to continue testing in laboratories, by computer, and with a zero yield. It means that using modern technology, they can make their nuclear weapons more sophisticated, despite a global ban on explosive tests.

The treaty is a charade. It does not deal with the nuclear danger as it exists and it does not ban all tests. The sinners are preaching to us the virtues of chastity.

Q: Is that India's only concern?

A: We also object strongly to a unique device in the proposed Comprehensive Test Ban Treaty which Britain, Russia and China insisted upon. We are told that we must sign so that the treaty can enter into force, whether we like it or not.

Q: The US has given an official assurance to India that it will not be punished with sanctions if it refuses to ratify the treaty. Why isn't that sufficient to satisfy Indian concerns?

A: We object to the kind of language that says we shall not be punished. We are not criminals. We are a sovereign nation. We have a right to decide. That apart, the treaty is a multilateral matter, not a bilateral matter. So the US assurance means nothing. That is what I told the US secretary of state when I wrote to him recently. If America feels an assurance is called for, why not amend the treaty?

153

Q: Is this an issue that is likely to sour relations between India and the US?
A: No. Indian foreign policy places a great deal of stress on friendship and cooperation with America. I am personally pleased that our relationship is progressing very well. Whatever our differences may be on this treaty issue, it does not affect in any way our bilateral relations.

Q: How else could the treaty be amended to take account of India's position?
A: The treaty should be linked to a timetable for general nuclear disarmament. Without that, India will not sign, nor will it give up its nuclear option. We are not going to test tomorrow. But surely it is a matter of legitimate security concern for us when we see around us powers which, either openly or clandestinely, are nuclear weapon states.

Q: Does India perceive a nuclear threat from China, Pakistan, or any other quarter?
A: I do not want to say so in so many words. But India's strategic planners would be unwise not to keep this in mind.

Q: When you say that India must keep its nuclear option open under present circumstances, does that mean it may need to carry out another nuclear explosive test, as it did in 1974?
A: It is not on our agenda in the immediate future. Since we last performed a test over 20 years ago, we have given a remarkable example of restraint which nobody else has done. Anybody else with such capability would have behaved differently. We will continue our restraint but not surrender our option.

Q: Does India have nuclear weapons already?
A: Not to my knowledge. I don't think we do so.

Q: Does India have the capability to build such weapons?
A: In today's world nothing is a secret. I don't think even our adversaries have credibly alleged that India has ever undertaken a nuclear weapon programme for we have not.

Thus to sum it up, the CTBT had always been visualized as the first definitive and irreversible step along the road to nuclear disarmament. It should have done so in two ways. First, the CTBT should have prohibited the designing and development of newer generations of nuclear weapons. Secondly, such a CTBT should have also signalled a shift in the perception of the nuclear weapon states who have sought to ensure their security through their nuclear arsenals for the last fifty years.

When the negotiations began we thought, somewhat optimistically, that the nuclear weapon states were ready to take such a first step on the road to nuclear disarmament. The negotiations have shown otherwise. It was a sad fact that the nuclear weapon states showed no interest in giving up their nuclear hegemony. The negotiations have ended without consensus because the text does not reflect the aspirations of the vast majority of countries for a nuclear weapon-free world. India was not alone in voicing these concerns. Many other countries also shared this conviction. It was a matter of regret that the Conference on Disarmament stopped negotiations on the CTBT to put forward a flawed text, to meet artificial deadlines, instead of taking advantage of the current moratorium on testing to continue negotiations for a universal CTBT that would meet the terms of the mandate.

It was also a fact that we had certain national security concerns which made it impossible for us to subscribe to a draft CTBT that is merely an instrument for horizontal non-proliferation rather than disarmament. Our security concerns obliged us to maintain our nuclear option. Yet, it was a fact that since we demonstrated our capability in 1974, we have exercised unpar-

155

alleled restraint. We have refrained from carrying out tests and from weaponizing our option. However, we could not accept constraints on our option as long as nuclear weapon states continued to rely on their nuclear arsenals for their security. Our position on the CTBT emerged out of an open and intense national debate that pointed out that the draft treaty would permit vertical proliferation by permitting tests by non-explosive means. Our policy reflected national consensus.

After we announced our decision that we could not subscribe to this draft Treaty, the Article on Entry into Force was modified suddenly with the clear aim of imposing obligations on India. This was at the insistence of a small number of countries. Such a provision was unprecedented in treaty negotiating practice and contrary to international legal norms. It denied India its sovereign right to exercise of consent and contained an element of implied coercion. It placed us in a position that we did not wish to be in. We were told that the text could not be modified but as we have seen, the draft text has been modified to accommodate one country's concerns. If this change had not been introduced or the Entry into Force provisions amended to address our concerns, we could have stood aside and let the draft text be adopted by those who supported it. But this attempt at coercion left us with no choice but to indicate our opposition to the draft text. Some friendly countries approached us with proposals of bilateral assurances with regard to this article. While we appreciate the spirit in which these gestures were made, we believe that in a multilaterally negotiated treaty, such private assurances did not address our concerns.

We were aware that some countries with which we have traditionally enjoyed close and mutually beneficial relations have adopted a different approach on the CTBT issue. We had in keeping with our practice, continued our dialogue with these countries in order to sensitise them to our concerns. Mutual respect implies respecting the right of sovereign nations to pursue their national interests even if there are differences of view. We are committed to developing and maintaining good relations with all countries and are confident that our differences on this issue would not affect our bilateral ties and friendly relations.

India has had a long-standing commitment to multilateralism. This has further accentuated today with the growing integration of our economy into global structures. We are increasingly engaged in our region. The Indian Ocean Rim Initiative and our membership of the ARF are developments that reflect acknowledgement of our constructive approach. In SAARC, we are trying to promote effective structures to enhance prosperity which can ensure stability in the region. India remains engaged in pursuing her policies for promoting peace, prosperity and stability and enhancing security in our region. We also continue to work with other countries to strive for achieving a nuclear weapon-free world.

157

17

India's Foreign Policy: An Overview

The Indian foreign policy, in the era of the post-Cold War period, made an effort to look at the current situation the world over, and tried to co-link it with the legacy that we had of the freedom struggle, along with the vision of future that we had for the twenty-first century.

We have every reason to feel proud of the way Indian democracy has consolidated itself in this half a century and the way our system is prospering. At the same time, in these years, we have also built some legacies, and the legacies are the foreign policies which were started by the great Nehru whose name we hold in great reverence. So far as the historical growth of this nation is concerned, the legacy was trying to correlate itself, as I said to what was going to happen in twenty-first century itself.

In the post-Cold War era, several new challenges are emerging before the world and our nation is no exception. The world order, which some powers are trying to spell out after the Cold War, is posing challenges for us. Hegemonism is once again confronting us. Those who think that they have the power to build the new order, have a great deal of disdain for all of us; they have disdain for the Third World, they have disdain for those who were not there in their midst when they were trying to build their own nations and, therefore, they were trying to build up some exclusive system for themselves. There were several forums, several exclusive clubs. One exclusive club was the Club P-7, comprising those who were nuclear weapon powers. There was another exclusive club which went by the name G-7 and it was a club of those who wanted to dominate through economic strength. But these powers, who were trying to monopolise a new world order, were also seeing that there were differences amongst themselves. For instance, the discussion that was going on in the European Security Conference in Lisbon, the unanimity that they were trying to present was no more available. We saw the Russian Prime Minister Viktor Chernomyrdin reject the view of the type of disarmament the others were spelling out. He said 'that enlargement of the North Atlantic Treaty Organisation would create a new and dangerous faultline between East and West at a time when the Continent should be striving to heal the old breach'. He also added: 'It is not clear that the appearance of a new dividing line would not lead to the worsening of the whole geo-political situation'.

All the same, in some areas we have noticed that when it came to us, they presented a different type of unity, often at our cost. Therefore, when we think in terms of nuclear powers, we should also think in terms of the attitude they have about the non-nuclear powers. They are powerful people; they wanted that all forums and all institutions which were built with effort ever since decolonization began, and ever since the new countries were becoming free, the platforms that they had built, should be demolished. One such platform was the NAM platform. Several people referred to NAM as being irrelevant. That was exactly what these powers wanted us to believe and we would be playing in their hands, if we start to feel that G-5 is relevant, G-7 is relevant or the P-5 is relevant but NAM is not.

NAM will continue to be relevant so long as we all have one interest to represent and that interest is the interest of the deprived, the interest of the ex-colonies.

159

Often we have been exposed to the various types of theories which they were trying to present to us—I mean the powerful ones—which were actually the treaties which were taking the countries of the world in one direction. It was a charade. One such charade was the NPT. Another charade was what was called the CTBT. Who defined these treaties? The NPT was signed. We did not sign it. I think, we refused for correct principled reasons. We felt it was an unequal treaty. We felt it was something which did not really mean to stop proliferation. Who defined it? Who performed the tests? Those very people who had signed the treaties started testing again almost the day after signing the treaty. The same was the case with CTBT. Who defined the CTBT? This had to be kept in mind all the time. Therefore, when we think in terms of a nuclear power, we should keep in mind this angle that the deception of CTBT and NPT was something which had been inflicted on us.

Consider what is happening to our industrial economy. I think that all those who were trying to give us a new economic order, were trying to spell it in the name of the Dunkel Award. We had discussed the Dunkel Award at length in our Parliament and also the WTO's new constitution. We had our doubts and our suspicions. I had the privilege of chairing the Committee which examined the general agreement on Tariffs and Trade in detail. When we examined it (GATT), we said that though we were joining it, we would always be vigilant.

The Government of India's Cabinet had taken a decision that so far as our vital interests were concerned, if any non-trade elements were being introduced, India would take a firm stand on that. I can assure you that under no circumstances did India give in.

When we talk in terms of the CTBT or when we talk in terms of the NPT or the economy or anything, the foremost interest that we have to safeguard is our own interest and that interest—is an enlightened self-interest—we know, is our future and, therefore, when we take a stand we abide by it. It was in this context, therefore, that whenever the issue of the CTBT arose we tried to see the writing on the wall where our legacy beckons us to respond, to preserve our Independence, preserve the independence of the Indian foreign policy and face with courage and fortitude all those challenges we were faced with. We are not an arrogant nation. We have never wanted confrontation. In the last fifty years or so various Prime Ministers have occupied these benches from Jawaharlal Nehru onwards. One of the things which is always evident is India's grit to stand up when challenges are posed before her. In this context, therefore, when we reacted to the CTBT we were reacting in the correct sense. I must say again, which I have said earlier, that when unitedly we refused to sign the CTBT, therein lay the power of India's glory. Yet many people told us that we would be isolated. Many pressures tried to influence us and yet we did not bend. At the same time, we kept in mind the fact that we all knew that there was a price for this defiance. Defiance was not going to be tolerated by those who had arrogance of power and wanted to spell out a new world order which was very different from our own vision. Therefore, they first tried to degrade us and then pressurise us. Pressures in the modern times, are never direct. There are a lot of hidden hands which are working all the time. These hidden hands have only one objective and that is to break the unity which the defiant nations exhibit.

How did they do it? By sapping our morale first. All the time—I have had due respect for the media, particularly the electronic media which has a universal and global appeal—we were told by them that we have done something wrong and we must find a way to get out of it. The CTBT, as laid down in the United Nations, said that there was a three-year period in which we must sign before the 'Entry into Force' clause becomes operative. In these three years, several things could have happened. One of those things which was happening was dangling of carrots and also wielding of the rod and I think, that the rod also manifests itself in many forms. Why did we lose the Security Council seat? Was it not a 'punishment'? Was it not a rod that was being shown to us? While responding to the debate on the CTBT, I said the same thing. I said: Ultimately, when we have made up our minds, when the nation has made up its mind that it is not going to compromise on such issues, then, whatever comes in our way, we will take and we will take it with dignity.

I had also said: 'The media propaganda is coming from outside. And now, in the modern sense, when the electronic media has become so powerful, I think that is where the response cannot come from the Government alone. The response can come from all of us together that we would not let an atmosphere prevail in the country that the media, insider or outsider, can cause confusion in our minds.

A nation cannot be defended with weak nerves. The safeguarding of a nation's interest needs more courage. When we are fighting a battle, we cannot ensure that every victory will be ours. I could not promise it. I could promise only one thing that I would uphold the mandate given to me by the Parliament unanimously. Basically, what was the mandate? The mandate was, to stand up with dignity. The mandate was to preserve the dignity of the Parliament and its legacy regardless of the fact whether we get a temporary seat or a permanent seat on the UN Security Council. Efforts were being made to see that India did not get a permanent seat. Several formulae were going around. One such formula was, while Japan and Germany would be admitted, the rest would be considered later. From the very beginning it was a fight against Japan. We knew that it was a powerful nation. From the very beginning we knew that Japan's resources were far larger than ours. The Government preceding our's decided to contest the decision. When we came into office, the preceding Government wrote to me and it is on record that we should not withdraw, and I honoured that.

162

We were often asked whether India should lead NAM or whether it should not do so. Leadership is not contesting elections alone; leadership is not asking for garlands. Real leadership surfaces at the time of difficulty when you have to take a stand. It was a proud moment when instead of just three we had forty nations supporting our decision regarding the CTBT and our claim to be awarded a non-permanent seat on the Security Council. I would like to repeat that three of the five nuclear-power States saw it advantageous to support us. The nation's interest is above everything. Therefore, when we fought the election, we fought with open eyes. The option was not between winning and losing. The option was between either withdrawing or contesting.

As far as foreign policy was concerned, we were trying to involve all the parties in every forum. To every forum we send a composite delegation. If we had started having a partisan attitude, it would not have sustained us.

There was a shift in the policy of China. I was quite conscious of the fact that the situation was such that our territory was in their possession. There was no doubt about that. That is what we were trying to discuss with them. There are always two options in the world—either go to war or discuss. And we had chosen for good reasons to discuss. Gradually, we were moving in one direction and that direction had not been built only by me; it had been built by several people. In 1976, when Atal Behari Vajpayee went to Beijing, he was building in that direction as well. In 1988, when Rajiv Gandhi went there, he made some inroads. Narasimha Rao did the same thing. And now we were trying to do the same and therein lies the real greatness of this country, that with the change of governments we do not change policies and directions of policies. That did not mean that we were rigid or stagnant; it did not mean that we did not take into account all the changes that were confronting us.

Mr Jyoti Basu did not go to Bangladesh to negotiate a treaty.

He had not finalized any arrangement. I think it is a great strength of India that in this democratic system, we use all parties, all our forces, whenever we need them in a particular given situation. It is primarily because we feel that when the question of the nation comes, we are all one. If Jyoti Basu's going to Bangladesh could help us in smoothening differences, why not? We are all Indians. We are all patriots. We are all committed to India's interests and, therefore, we all have to act together. The Indian foreign policy was taken a step further when all the SAARC Foreign Ministers met in India to discuss as to how we could go further on South Asian Preferential Trade Agreement (SAPTA) South Asian Free Trade Agreement (SAFTA) and on other political questions. The vision of SAFTA was before us. The credit of constructing SAFTA goes to the government in power before us.

It has been the good luck of India and again by the previous government's efforts, we were able to have the full dialogue partnership with the countries on the other side, i.e. the ASEAN countries. We were also trying to build our regional cooperation. We were trying to work closely with the ASEAN countries and the Asian Regional Forum (ARF). On the other side, we were constructing our relationship in the Indian Ocean region, fourteen countries of the Indian Ocean region, i.e. from Australia, Africa, including two countries of ASEAN were forming an association. These fourteen nations' combination were trying to build a common market.

We have a number of reasons to be proud of our cooperation with South Africa. South Africa is also a part of the Indian Ocean Rim countries and a part of NAM. I have had the privilege of talking to the Deputy President of South Africa. He reiterated his firm faith in the NAM movement and he said that they wanted to host the next NAM summit in South Africa. NAM must never be looked at, in those terms that the Western powers want us to look at it.

In Afghanistan, the Taliban was reigning. We have to ask ourselves that who were helping the Taliban? Taliban did not drop from the sky. They were from some country. They were trained in some country. They acquired arms from some country. They had been sustained by some countries. And the identity of those countries are pretty obvious to all of us. We knew who was doing the damage. And India had to stand up. India's stand in this situation has been different, not due to a fault of ours but because of the nature of the events. The Minister of Agriculture came to my rescue when I was not well and he went to Teheran to attend the first conference held there regarding Afghanistan. The role that he played was very commendable, he upheld India's tradition. That also helped to project that the foreign policy was not the monopoly of the Foreign Minister. All of us were a part of it.

India's policy regarding Pakistan is not polemical. Pakistan has been trying to isolate us but contrarily, has been getting itself isolated. That is why when Benazir Bhutto, former Prime Minister of Pakistan spoke in the United Nations, I did not respond to her. I did not want to enter into polemical problems because that did not serve any purpose. It is only a sheer pretense.

I was asked to snap diplomatic relations with Pakistan. It was not a correct approach. Even in 1962, when we had that unfortunate incident in relation to China, we did not close our embassy. Embassies, basically, are our ears and eyes. They are more important in adverse circumstances than in helpful situations. It is very easy to withdraw and bring everyone back home and keep them at safe distances from very difficult spots. But it's important that when the circumstances are difficult, our missions should be there.

We explained our position regarding CTBT repeatedly. I had written to every Foreign Minister of the world twice. We had also instructed our Ambassadors to go to their Foreign Offices and explain our stand in detail. This campaign, which had to be sustained by India, did not end there because we still had three years within which to decide. Therefore, in those years in between, we had to sustain our campaign. We also wanted to redefine the role of NAM because in the post-Cold War era it would need to play a radically different role.

No foreign policy or security policy of a country can be constructed without this institutional back-up from the Parliament. For quite a long time, we had depended either on the structured bureaucracy or on the whims, wills or faculties of one individual minister or the other. Political leadership should have a vision; only then can it assert itself, political leadership has to have a commitment; only then can it assert itself and political leadership does not mean 'individuals,' it means, 'institutionalization' and that is why we were moving towards institutionalization so that we were able to project India's strength through the policies that we followed.

We reserve our options regarding the nuclear issue. I think it means a lot. If it had not meant a lot, then the pressure to sign would not have been so strong. The decision whether to sign or not was not an individual one. This is something to be decided by those who have the responsibility in regard to the defense strategy of the country. It should be decided by those who have been entrusted with the responsibility of assessing threats to our national security from time to time. Weapons of any type to be built or not built, to be acquired or not acquired—should be left to them.

In regard to Bangladesh and the Chakma problem, I had visited Bangladesh and discussed it. The response was very positive and helpful. I think that was the real essence of our relationship with the government then in Bangladesh which was that, on issues of contention, we were trying to find areas of agreement and co-operation.

166

18

Price of an Independent Foreign Policy*

The Foreign Policy of every country is integrally linked with its history and its basic ethos. Our republic is now half a century old. Fifty years ago, the Indian Foreign Policy was perceived on the basis of our experiences and the promises made during the freedom struggle.

A unique feature of the Gandhian struggle was its non-violent character and intimate linkage with the anti-Apartheid struggle of the African people. Gandhi himself had courageously resisted discrimination, which was one of the basic tenets of the foreign policy of free India.

The freedom struggle not only spelt out the future of India but also visualized how India would cope with the international situation. India was, at that time, confronted with the reality of the Cold War between the blocs. Today we might talk of Non-Alignment as a concept. In Nehru's vision—or call it the legacy of the freedom struggle—one thing was certain that no country could consider itself free till its foreign policy was liberated from any commitment to one or the other bloc.

At the time of India's freedom—the Non-Aligned world came much later—India had stated that it was not going to be a part of

---

*Speech in the Parliament on 17/12/1996.

any bloc. Both the blocs condemned us. Stalin called Nehru 'the running dog of imperialism' and what John Foster Dulles said about India can be read in books. It is in that context, therefore, that Nehru as the first Foreign Minister of India said that we did not want to join any bloc. In a way he was not talking of any bloc but of India being free to make its choice. Non-alignment has only one meaning and that is the freedom of choice. Each country should judge its own national interest and then decide what it wants to do. Nehru did not want either Moscow or Washington to decide our Foreign Policy. Today, we may term the decision as good or bad but the basic point is that a free India or a Republic could not have any other Foreign Policy—even if it has to relive its past. This was a challenge which the mighty did not like. But gradually, as the decolonization process advanced and country after country became free they all shared this viewpoint.

Nehru did not go around asking people to join the Non-Aligned Movement. The former colonies realized that when a country sheds off the yoke of colonialism it has to perceive the paradigms of its foreign policy, i.e. what kind of a relationship it would have with rest of the world. A large number of countries, more than one hundred at that time which were independent, realised that if they remained under the thumb of one bloc or the other, their freedom, would be compromised. That is why the Non-Aligned Movement expanded.

With the end of the Cold War, the animosities between the blocs ended. Suddenly, we saw the pendulum moving in another direction. The designs of established hegemonies, be they in the economic field, in politics or in foreign policy were exceedingly oppressive. Some countries would like to keep the world under their thumb. Certain associations were formed; calling themselves G-7 and P-5. They might have differences among themselves but so far as hegemony over the Third World was concerned, it was a shared objective. That is why when we talk

168

in terms of our own future, and when we talk in terms of what we have to do, we have to perceive it as a challenge, particularly our concepts of freedom of choice. It is important for us to keep in mind that in the economic sphere, we are confronted with the G-7 and the P-5.

As far as the nuclear NPT or CTBT goes, we did not sign these because they were flawed. Who defied the agreements after signing the CTBT? Who did the test? Not those who did not sign it. France signed it, broke it; China signed it, broke it. Even the CTBT was drafted with certain reservations that permitted certain type of tests. This was our basic objection. We were asking them to make it more candid.

It was a matter of pride that in face of such challenges, the nation stood united. We all felt that India's freedom was at stake and we should safeguard our interests. We anticipated some punishments to follow. All the same, we stood up and I am glad that we did so. But signing the CTBT or not signing it did not end the story in September, 1996. The first punishment that followed was our defeat in the Security Council. Was it ever perceived that we could abstain and we would defy them and yet we would get elected to the Security Council?

It must be known clearly as to who decides which candidate is best suited for a permanent membership of the Security Council. Not the common vote, definitely not by the vote of Africa or Asia. Basically, powers are centralised and they would not let us sit in the Security Council after our defiance. For every defiance, we have to pay a price and all those nations who want to stand on their own feet, must learn how to stand up and defy. Defiance is unavoidable if we are to assert our independence.

Pressures in the modern world are never direct. Gunboat diplomacy has had its day. Pressures are now applied through indirect methods, which are called lobbies. Lobbies are built for that purpose and lobbyists have their own methods of functioning. We must understand the operational skills of the lobbyists to fully comprehend the nature of the pressures being applied on us.

Our morale must not get sapped at losing this seat. After all, it has happened in the past also. We were once defeated by Pakistan in 1975. President Clinton has on record said that India would sign. That India would come around. That was the challenge to us. Would India have come around? Did India want to come around? Was it in India's interest to come around? Was it consistent with our self-respect to come around? Was it consistent with our legacy to come around? If it was not, then let us make our position very clear. All this is part and parcel of the same situation. A defeat is also a method of a well-orchestrated pressure and an inadequate resistance.

China, Russia and France stood by us, despite the pressure. By the time, the question of the Security Council came in, we had forty supporters. How did that happen? After all, increasingly, it was realized that whether it was the issue of CTBT or anything else, pressure had to be resisted. When we had forty supporters, it was very interesting to note the fact that out of the five nuclear powers, three voted with us. Why did they vote with us? Each one of them had its own compulsions. China had its own reasons; Russia had its own reasons; and France had its own reasons.

Therefore, when we refer to the post-Cold War, the CTBT is only one of the major unresolved issues that continues to confront us. In the post-Cold War era, it is regional cooperation that is most important, because there is no country in the world which is not concentrating on regional cooperation. Europe is talking of Europeans; America is talking in terms of Mexico and Canada; Latin Americans have their own regional cooperation, Africans have their own and so do we.

In the area of regional cooperation, our concept was not confined only to South Asia. We were looking at a wider area—a neighbourhood does not only mean geographical proximity. It pertains to interest proximity as well. Interest may not be 100 per cent similar, we need to work out the highest common factor which facilitated our joining the full dialogue partnership with the ASEAN. We could not join it earlier because of the compulsions of the Cold War, wherein every country of the ASEAN had one commitment or the other. In the post-Cold War era, our joining as a full dialogue partner of ASEAN is of benefit to us.

The other dimension of Indian foreign policy was Central Asia. With Central Asia, we have age old relations. In our history, we had good relations with the Buddhist, the Kushan and the Mughal Central Asia. We have been trying to reorient these relations. These countries are rich in petroleum. In the twenty-first century, 40 per cent of available energy is perceived to be consumed in Asia, more than half of it by China and India together. Naturally, all eyes are turning to Central Asia. The politics of the next few years is going to be the politics of gas pipelines and that is where India's relationship with these countries would matter. We have, to an extent, succeeded in restructuring our relations with Iran. In the previous era, we exported goods to Central Asia via Odessa in the Soviet era. This is a very circuitous route. We look forward to facilitate trade and enhance our relations.

Iran has also undergone a major change. In 1990, I recall when I was a Minister, I was to go to Iran for an official visit. One week before my visit, the visit was officially cancelled by Iran on the plea that they were in sympathy with the suffering Muslims in Kashmir. The same Iran, the same Mr Velayati, has come twice to invite India to participate in the Afghanistan Conference in Iran despite Pakistan Minister's telling them that if India was invited they would not come. Iran did not care. India was there, India was present at the Afghanistan Conference in New York. This was a new orientation of the Indian Foreign Policy.

We are a factor in the Afghanistan situation although we did not want to interfere. We do not want to enter into any arms race in Afghanistan. We want a peaceful Afghanistan. We are strongly averse to the growth of blatant fundamentalism in our close neighbourhood. That is one of the reasons why we had continued to recognize the Rabbani regime. We had good relations with Dostum and Masood. This was a new type of Afghan policy that we sorted out and pursued. But the central point of the Indian Foreign Policy was SAARC. In 1996, India was the Chairman of SAARC. It was a good thing for us, a good feeling for us because SAARC was undergoing a postive change.

The birth of Bangladesh was a remarkable achievement for India. It was not solely the Indian Government's achievement, but a combined effort of India and Bangladesh. We must look at it in terms of a wider framework. We also had very good relations with Nepal. We had agreed to give them access to Bangladesh through India and the Mahakali Treaty was signed between India and Nepal during my tenure.

The Non-Aligned Movement was the major plank of Indian foreign policy. What could have been the alternative policy? What do we do if we do not want to stay with those who are like us, if we do not want to stay with those who have gone through the colonial era themselves, if we do not want to stay with those who are also against the hegemonism of some powers? Then who do we want to stay with? Do we want to stay with the hegemonists? Do we want to go to the doorsteps of those who want to exploit us, whose interests are known to us and which are not in our favour? Nehru had always said that we were not a bloc. We were a movement. The difference between a bloc and a movement is that you have the freedom of choice, sometimes voluntary, sometimes, non-voluntary. Not only this, autonomy of choice, and freedom of action is a central point of NAM, it is also something on which, a position of strength can be built. And that is what we had been trying to do.

The issue regarding our border with China has not been sorted out. We feel that through the proposed Confidence Building Measures (CBM), we could improve our relations. In 1993, Narasimha Rao went to Beijing, to tranquilize the border. We have taken that tranquility one step further. But their claims regarding the boundary remain unchanged. The new Sino-Indian mode is that although contentious issues remain, we are trying to work out cooperation in various areas.

We gave a shift to our policy towards a people-to-people relationship with Pakistan by issuing more visas—more visas were given to the divided families that had come to meet their family members here. Did India gain or lose? Most of these people come from Karachi. Why did Pakistan close down the consulate in Karachi? It was primarily because they wanted to hinder them from visiting India. Prior to closing of the Consulate, we were issuing 750 visas a day from Karachi alone. We were exerting our best to give as many visas as we could but the number did not exceed 300 because we did not have adequate manpower in our mission at Islamabad.

Sometimes many speculations are made regarding the Indo-Pak talks. But whenever we talk, I feel, we should talk on a strictly official level.

The thrust of the foreign policy that we were trying to pursue, if I may say broadly, was not reactive; it was active; we took initiatives. We had taken major initiatives regarding Bangladesh. We had taken major initiatives regarding Afghanistan. We had taken another major initiative regarding the Comprehensive Test Ban Treaty. We took initiatives regarding the ASEAN and, also to an extent and within a limited sphere, new initiatives regarding making our borders peaceful.

19

India's Foreign Policy in a
Changing World*

India's foreign policy is a mix of continuity and change. In broad
terms, it is built on the nation's consensus. The values that have
formed our identity, our Constitution and structured our polity,
have also guided our diplomacy.

The concept of Non-Alignment, our support for decolonization, the emphasis on democratization of international institutions,
a serious effort to move the world towards disarmament,
restructuring of the inequitable international economic and
information orders, and the global fight against racism—are the
concepts and policies that have had the support of our entire
nation.

In the 1990s, the world underwent momentous changes. Old
mindsets, ideologies, economic systems—gave way to new structures of thought, to new technologies, and to new ways of addressing problems inherited from history. A new world order
was in the process of evolving. There was greater openness,
diffusion of power, and an increasing realization that the security of nation-states was related to its economic growth, political
cohesion and democratic functioning. Military solutions were

*Address to the National Defence College on 16/10/1990.

becoming less and less viable. Political and institutional inter-dependence began increasingly characterizing international intercourse. Shared ecological and environmental concerns transcended national boundaries.

These developments cannot but have a major impact on the way we look at the world and the way we construct and exercise our foreign policy options. What, in this context, could be India's role? How should India's foreign policy priorities be fashioned against this background? The foreign policy of any nation-state is an integral part of its overall conceptual framework and flows out of the value system and objectives, all put together. Foreign policy provides the framework for achieving, essentially through peaceful means, our national objectives in the international arena. There can be no foreign policy separate from the overall strategy of the nation-state.

Nehru's great contribution to the evolution of our foreign policy was that he gave us a conceptual framework which was dynamic and which was based on a cooperative and peaceful alternative founded on the twin pillars of peaceful coexistence and non-violence. It is this conceptual framework that we must continue to adopt in evolving a foreign policy based on peace, security and cooperation in the world. Our first priority has been, and must continue to be, our immediate neighbours.

We pursued a policy that sought friendship and a mutually-beneficial cooperation with our neighbours, while at the same time safeguarding our security. There is much in a civilizational sense that unites us with our neighbours. We have had similar historical experiences and we share similar problems of economic development and technological modernisation. We are joined in a geographic sense as much as in our efforts to give our people a better life. Unless we and our neighbours in South Asia live together in a cooperative community of South-Asian nations, we will remain isolated from the global process of integration of national economies and production capabilities that will be one of the principal characteristics of the world of the next century.

Our efforts in improving relations with our neighbouring countries have met with considerable success, with the sole exception of Pakistan.

It can be said with confidence today that our efforts to transform the political climate in South Asia have met with a great measure of success. Clouds of suspicion which characterized our neighbours' perception of us, have largely disappeared. They have begun to see us as partners in constructive cooperation for mutual benefit.

In Sri Lanka, we were hopeful that the Sri Lankan Government will fulfil its promises of devolution of power and ensure the safety, security and democratic aspirations of their Tamil people. Amity between different people of Sri Lanka is beneficial not only for them, but would directly contribute to peace and stability in the region.

With Nepal, our relations are rooted in history. We welcomed the process of democratization in Nepal and wished the Nepalese people well in the great task of evolving their own polity and establishing their own traditions of democracy.

China is our most important neighbour with whom we have a shared commitment to enhancing cooperation in diverse fields and promoting a close dialogue on international issues. There was demonstrable reduction in tensions with China. We consulted each other more frequently on issues before international organizations. There is clear evidence of political will both in India and China to find a fair, reasonable and mutually acceptable settlement to the boundary question.

With Bangladesh, the Maldives and Bhutan, our traditionally friendly relations were further strengthened, and we were confident that a sound basis for a productive relationship had been established.

It is only with Pakistan that relations deteriorated. The responsibility for this lies squarely on Pakistan. Their perceptions go contrary to the larger global trend towards peace and cooperation. They chose a path of wilful interference in our internal affairs. We wished to normalize our relationship with Pakistan and live as friendly neighbours. People who have old and outmoded mindsets who refuse to learn from history, or have vested interests that seek perpetuation of their own dominance within Pakistan's polity, are the only ones who can contemplate such a horrible animosity.

We offered a package of measures to induce mutual confidence and cooperation. But regrettably, Pakistan has chosen to ignore them and persists in its unacceptable activities. Our territorial integrity is not negotiable. For the rest, we have the political will and a publicly stated commitment to establish friendly and co-operative relations with Pakistan.

We attached great importance to the strengthening of the South Asian Association for Regional Cooperation (SAARC), for we believe that regional organizations have acquired an added relevance in promoting international cooperation. We were committed to a steady expansion of its activities and looked forward to Afghanistan and a democratic Myanmar joining this organization to work for our collective prosperity.

The crisis in the Gulf was very much on all our minds. There has been some misrepresentation about India's position. We, on our part, had no doubts. India's position was, and remains, clear and consistent. The crisis had arisen from the Iraqi invasion of Kuwait. We firmly oppose aggression. Therefore, we urged Iraq to withdraw its forces from Kuwait, as demanded by the Security Council. We did not recognize Kuwait's annexation.

India fully subscribes to and strictly abides by, all the resolutions of the Security Council concerning this crisis. But, at the same time, we believed that all efforts had to be made to achieve a peaceful political solution of the crisis.

The crisis led to the induction of foreign forces into the Gulf region. In the changed world environment, a permanent foreign military presence is not desirable in any country, nor would it be in anyone's interest.

In responding to the rapidly-changing world and in looking ahead, India must seek sustenance from the value system that has defined its civilizational identity and constituted the philosophical foundations of its stability. With about one-sixth of the world population, the seventh largest landmass in the world, a rich base of natural resources, a continental economy, a pool of trained manpower and a strategic location astride the Indian Ocean, India has obvious and undeniable inherent strengths. India is too populous and too large, not to conceive of an independent and legitimate role for itself. This is a necessary consequence of our sovereignty and political autonomy. We do not subscribe to the doctrine of balance of power. We do not accept great power chauvinism which seeks spheres of influence, wants other nations' resources at dictated prices, or aims to play the role of an universal ideologue. India seeks to play a legitimate role consistent with its inherent strength and its commitment to the immutable values of freedom, democracy, secularism and economic interdependence. When the world is gradually moving away from conflict and confrontation to dialogue, mutual understanding and cooperation, India is uniquely placed to make a useful contribution.

In suggesting a cooperative and peaceful alternative based on political independence and an acceptance of ideological and systemic diversity, our foreign policy has sought to project an alternative path away from confrontation and violence. Ours is not an idealistic pursuit of unattainable goals. Our foreign policy is pragmatic and designed to further our national interests within the framework of a peaceful world.

One of the major developments of this century has been the growth of a universal consciousness that despite all its diversity, shows a level of global concerns which transcend partisan, regional and parochial interests. We in India are acutely aware of our responsibilities, and indeed of the seriousness with which these global concerns need to be addressed. Consistent with our integrated view of humankind and society, we are convinced that issues clustered around the global concerns of decolonization, development, disarmament and democratisation, must receive the urgent attention of the world community. Developmental concerns must address themselves to the removal of economic disparities, to promises in evolving a new and more equitable economic order, proposals for financial and monetary reforms, North-South negotiations, South-South cooperation, and considered plans of action for the removal of global want and poverty.

Looking at the world today, there are some positive and hopeful trends that characterize global activity—steps towards disarmament, evidence of openness, reducing emphasis on rigid ideology, and a greater stress on institutional interdependence. There is a growing awareness of the interrelationship between economic development and environmental protection, and there is greater evidence of democratization. These are positive developments and we shall, as our foreign policy priority, endeavour to further them in cooperation with the international community.

But, on the negative side, there are disturbing trends that we must take careful note of. There are trends towards accentuation of economic disparity, restriction on transfer of essential technologies, protectionism, reduced and discriminatory aid flows, increasing recourse to unilateral and coercive measures to gain commercial objectives; a frightening spurt in international terrorism and an enhanced brutalization of society. Narco-terrorism and its linkages with fundamentalism, are becoming an international scourge. Environmental degradation and ecological damage have already aroused grave concerns. Much of these damages are inflicted through over-consumption and greed in more privileged parts of the globe.

179

It is against this backdrop, and in the light of major historical changes that the world is undergoing, that we must view the challenges posed before us. As a developing country, our basic objective is to ensure an improvement in the conditions of living of our people and to break through the bonds of poverty. This can only be done through putting our economy on a path of accelerated growth, technological change and modernization, while at the same time reducing disparities and eliminating social injustices. This is the only way to go if India is to occupy her rightful place in the world. To achieve this, we must persevere in pursuing the middle way of synthesis between ancient beliefs and progressive changes. For this, peace is a necessary precondition. To institutionalize international peace, a re-affirmation of our faith in the principles of tolerance, diversity, pluralism and democracy, is essential. We must evolve a foreign policy that is rooted in our national priorities, but which simultaneously furthers India's contribution to a peaceful, democratic, and economically interdependent world order, sensitive to global concerns that transcend national boundaries. This is the task before us, and this is what we shall continue to work for in the years ahead.

III

REGIONAL COOPERATION

20

The Importance of Regional Cooperation*

In this age of globalization, nations in different parts of the world have discovered the advantages of regional economic cooperation and the benefits of a common regional economic space. At the end of World War II, who would have imagined that France and Germany, who had fought three bitter wars in the preceding 80 years, would come together to create the European Community, which has now become the European Union. Nearer to us, countries of South East Asia have been able to achieve commendable success in development with regional cooperation with ASEAN playing a key role in this process. In America, both NAFTA and Mercosur (or the Southern Cone Common Market) reflect the same economic imperative.

The prospects of forging closer ties of economic cooperation in our region improved perceptibly during my tenure as Prime Minister. There was an increasing convergence in our macro economic policies, with an emphasis on deregulation and a greater role for the private sector. All of us were seeking to unleash the creative energies of our entrepreneurs and workers and increase

---

*Speech by Prime Minister of India on Bangla-India-Pakistan Business Summit—Dhaka, 15/1/1998.

our productive efficiency so that we could compete more effectively in the globalised economy. We saw a quickening of growth in our individual economies with increases in GNP ranging from 5 to 7 per cent. There was no reason why we could not sustain and accelerate this pace of growth with sound economic management and by capitalizing on regional cooperation.

Economic Cooperation was high on the SAARC agenda. The goal of achieving a Free Trade Area in South Asia was accepted, and the timeframe to achieve it advanced to the year 2001. Our commitment to work jointly to achieve this goal was reaffirmed. This would involve progressive acceleration of trade liberalization in the SAPTA negotiations in terms of the products covered, the depth of the tariff cuts and lifting of non-tariff barriers. In concrete terms, we were required to liberalize at least 25 per cent of trade each year to usher in a Free Trade Area in South Asia by the first year of the next century.

Under the first two rounds of SAPTA, India offered the maximum concessions covering around 1000 tariff lines. We also offered the most number of tariff cuts with special concessions to the least developed countries.

India was committed to expediting SAPTA liberalization. It was prepared to lift quantitative restrictions on agreed items of interest for Bangladesh and other least developed SAARC countries. Our negotiators had the requisite mandate to reduce tariffs more significantly with deeper cuts for Bangladesh and the least developed SAARC countries as part of the latest round of trade preference talks. All this imparted the required momentum to the SAPTA liberalization process. Our SAARC partners, particularly Bangladesh, also had an added opportunity to access our market and enhance their exports to India.

The achievement of a Free Trade Area in South Asia not only provided a stimulus to trade and investment within the region, but also made the region a more attractive destination for foreign investors. With an enlarged regional market of more than one billion people, the SAARC partners acquired greater weight and significance in their global and regional strategies. To encourage Indian entrepreneurs to invest in South Asia, the Indian government had decided to double the ceiling for overseas Indian investment in this region.

Today, trade liberalization alone is not sufficient for expansion of trade and investment. We have to speed up our arrangements for trade facilitation. Meaningful initiatives were taken by SAARC in this direction. Given our common administrative background, it was planned to quickly work out conformance and harmonization arrangements in areas such as customs procedures, standards and quality, and electronic data exchange leading to paperless trade, which would help reduce transaction costs and make intra-SAARC trade more efficient and prosperous for business.

Limitations in physical infrastructure acted as a brake on the growth of trade. Intra-regional transportation and communication links remained weak. Improvements in these sectors were critical if we wanted to derive the full benefits of geographical proximity. We needed to identify additional routes by road and rail, augment air links and look at ways to reduce freight costs by sea. Infrastructure also required upgradation and development. India was prepared to work with its neighbours in identifying and undertaking joint projects, both short-term and long-term, to improve and upgrade transport facilities. We wanted to develop the capacity to not only handle the anticipated expansion of trade within the region but also connect to the proposed trans-Asian transport networks. Our region is strategically situated at the crossroads of Asia, between the oil-rich countries in West and Central Asia and the dynamic economies of South East Asia. We should make full use of this geographical advantage.

As an immediate measure, India was prepared to double the number of freight trains from India to Pakistan from the existing level of 10–15 trains a month to one everyday. We also offered to increase the frequency of the Samjhauta Express, which was running twice a week from India to Pakistan, to six times a week. This was not only in keeping with our commitment to make travel easy within the region and promote greater contact between our peoples, but was also intended to signal our resolve to move forward in practical ways.

Regional cooperation was no longer driven only by exchange of commodities and manufactures. We, therefore, wanted to establish tradability of some key resources that our region is richly endowed with, and to complement each other in economic development. Only then would South Asian economic cooperation lead to significant trade creating a growth generating impact. We wanted to make arrangements on a bilateral or tri-lateral basis to enable and facilitate such exchanges in key resources like electricity, natural gas, etc. We also found that our private sectors were very interested in this endeavour as were international funding agencies and foreign investors. India, for one, provides a large and virtually inexhaustible market for many of these resources. I offered to optimally harness these resources through concrete projects involving joint ventures, both at government and private sector levels, and we were also prepared to import goods from our neighbours for mutual benefit. As a first step towards regional cooperation in the field of energy, I proposed that SAARC undertake a study on the possibility of a Regional Electricity Grid.

On international trade issues, there is so much that our countries could do together, because we have common concerns and expectations from the existing WTO regime. Even on new issues, there was a striking convergence in our views and approaches. So SAARC became an interest group within the group of developing countries, pressing for a development-friendly orientation to the International Trading System. Trade and industry also coordinated their thinking and provided inputs to help us evolve a South Asian view of the WTO.

The private sector has played an important role in the common endeavour to expand trade and commercial links and accelerate economic growth in our region. We commend the work done by the SAARC Chamber of Commerce and Industry in throwing up ideas, posing ambitious targets and forging a consensus. It was heartening that we can count on the full support of our business communities in building the framework for economic cooperation in our region. Indeed, they did take the lead in evolving concrete proposals for mutually beneficial business cooperation which transcended the goal of a Free Trade Area and envisaged a South Asian Economic Community with the free movement of capital, goods and services within the region.

We stand at the threshold of a new century. The twentieth century saw us attain political independence, an epoch-making event that triggered the end of colonialism across the world. I am confident that, in the twenty-first century, our region will successfully overcome poverty and usher in an era of prosperity. Our products will once again be recognized for their excellence, even as our workers will be prized for their skill and ingenuity. We require statesmanship, vision and perseverance in fully harnessing the synergies that would flow from regional economic cooperation if we are to fulfill this promise.

I am reminded here of a verse from the Rig Veda, one of the oldest treatises of the Indian subcontinent. It says:

May you walk in step together,
May you speak in one voice,
May your minds unite in knowledge.

I hope we can keep these simple words in the back of our minds even as we strive together for a brighter tomorrow for our people.

21

South Asian Cooperation*

For developing countries, nothing is more important in today's world than building bilateral and multilateral relations amongst neighbours.

Often it is forgotten that the decolonization process had gathered momentum in the midst of the Cold War, which influenced the foreign and domestic policies of the developing countries. Non-Alignment was conceptualized and crafted by India and some other like-minded countries to protect and promote the independence and sovereignty of developing nations from the global thrusts of the Cold War.

With the end of Cold War, it became necessary for us, and the other developing countries, to appraise afresh our positions and forge new linkages with the World.

We have to understand the directions and meaning of the emerging realities and keep in step with the change without losing our national moorings. With the predictable certainties of the Cold War gone, the international and inter-State relations have become more complicated. There are challenges and also great opportunities for our countries. Mindsets of the Cold War era had kept us as distant neighbours of each other. With the

*Speech delivered at the Conference of Peace, Asia and South Asia on 27/7/1990.

end of this era, our interactions started improving and we have reasons to derive some satisfaction from this.

We in South Asia were hamstrung by underdevelopment. Absence of direct air links despite the SAARC agreements, remained an inhibiting factor. Of late, there is some improvement in telecommunications. Trade and economic relations amongst the countries of the region are still limited. We see the neighbouring ASEAN group doing much better. It is time that we, the South Asians, learnt from the South-East Asians example of cooperation where every member of the ASEAN has benefited a great deal from the regional cooperation.

The United Front government tried to build a new milieu of peace and friendship. In our election manifesto, we had assigned priority to South Asian friendship, as doing so would guide the region towards global change. All that was required was dialogue, understanding and cooperation. The government's first priority, therefore, was to normalize relations with the neighbours. In the relatively short period of six months, we succeeded in normalizing relations with Bangladesh and Nepal, and in removing from the India-Sri Lanka relationship, the abrasive load of the presence of the IPKF in Sri Lanka. Though the renewed fighting between LTTE and the armed forces of Sri Lanka did create anxieties and concerns for us about another refugee influx, we regarded the main issue to be Sri Lanka's internal problem and did not want to intervene in its internal affairs. Despite these worries our relations with Sri Lanka were better than at any time since 1983 and we hoped to build wider economic relations between our two countries in the years to come.

I wish we had been able to turn a new leaf in our relations with Pakistan. We were ready to open a new forward-looking dialogue with Pakistan and to offer Pakistan our hand of genuine good neighbourliness. But the Government of Pakistan mistakenly sees the political trouble in Kashmir as an opportunity to wrest the valley. The whole world is aware of how Pakistan is feeding terrorism in Kashmir and thus grossly intervening in our domestic affairs. Despite this, we maintain our desire to normalize relations with our immediate neighbour.

We in South and South-East Asia share the explosive problem of ethnopolitical overflows. In multinational societies, ethnopolitical issues are becoming inflammable. In South Asia, India shares borders with five nations, including a water border with Sri Lanka. However, most of us in South Asia have major ethnopolitical problems to deal with; even those who do not have these problems today may confront them in future. How can any one of us afford to take advantage of domestic problems and domestic difficulties of our neighbours?

Indeed, what we need in South Asia is to build a cluster of principles around which good neighbourliness can be built on an enduring basis.

The National Front Government was trying to build the foundations of basic principles of inter-state relations. We gave solemn assurances to Sri Lanka and Bangladesh that we would not allow Indian territory to be used against those countries. With Nepal, the open borders were borders of friendship; trade and human beings enjoy easy access across it without hindrance. Indeed, Nepal is a textbook case of how a strained relationship can be transformed into a relationship of mutual trust and confidence with goodwill on both sides and determination to let friendship do what unfriendliness could never do, namely, promote cooperation on the basis of equal mutual advantage.

Numerous questions are posed to the ruling elites of Pakistan. Do they really believe that they can capture Indian territory by force or subversion? Does hostility with India truly serve the interests of the Pakistan State and people? Is a policy of hostility and subversion not against the trend and process of global change? Will it help them to build democratic foundations, restore peace and order in their conflicted provinces and bring about a greater social equilibrium in a highly disjointed society? Or should we not work together to overcome our common problems and harness our considerable resources to give the great mass of poor people in our respective countries a better future?

The Government of Pakistan was asked to address a question that they have avoided all these years: what is the impulse that comes in their way of living with India in a peaceful neighbourly coexistence? May I ask them to remove from their minds any doubt they may have nourished, all these years without any evidence, that Indians do not accept Pakistan as a sovereign political reality? May I reiterate what has been stated by many Indians in authority that India wishes the Pakistani State well, that it is in the Indian interest that Pakistan be a strong, united, sovereign, democratic state, friendly towards India and other neighbours on terms of mutual and equal benefits.

If Pakistanis were to spell out their perceptions of friendship with India, I can assure them that we would give it attention and sympathy. Of course, they cannot expect us to give up our territory or modify our secular system or allow them to intervene in our domestic affairs. Also, we cannot permit growth of any kind of fundamentalism on our own soil.

We have more than a million Muslims, who constitute an integral part of our diverse nation. Their contribution in strengthening the Indian nation state is second to none and the inputs of Islam in the country's civilization has made it rich and proud. We take pride in saying that we are the world's second largest Muslim country that derives strength from its secularism and democracy. The fundamentalists, I say with regret, do not care for the welfare of the millions of Muslims of India nor for the Muslims of Xiangtan China or of those in the Central Asian Republics. If Pakistan is willing to sit down with us in India to thrash out a modus operandi of peaceful co-existence of the two neighbours, it can be a constructive exercise.

India has attached importance to SAARC and hopes that it

191

will grow into a viable and vibrant organization of regional co-operation. South Asia as a geopolitical region, is vastly different from ASEAN. It is much larger in area and population and more diverse in culture. South-East Asia is a high-growth region; the economy of the ASEAN group is one of the most dynamic in the world today. Cooperation between India and the ASEAN countries has increased significantly. We have friendly relations with Indonesia, Singapore, Malaysia, Thailand and the Philippines. With each of these countries, our trade and other economic relations are expanding steadily. India's joint ventures in the ASEAN countries are doing well; a positive development, in this respect, is the increasing interest taken by the private enterprises in expanding economic cooperations.

The South-East Asian region is in the process of rapid integration with the larger region of Asia-Pacific, of which India too is a part. We cannot afford to fall behind global trends and processes. We have to leave the past behind us. We must look at the present as the road to a future of mutual cooperation in peace and friendship.

192

22

Significance of Good Neighbourly Relations*

Mutually beneficial relationships amongst neighbours are of supreme importance. Let us recall that the anti-colonial struggles of various countries were in a way, inter-linked. After decolonization, NAM was conceptualized and crafted by India and other countries to collectively safeguard our sovereignties. As the Cold War ended, the developing countries appraised their interests in the 'New World Order' where the adversaries of yesteryears became friends and partners.

The concept of 'One European Home' is no longer a rainbow dream; it is a political reality. The industrially developed nations are integrating their economies and technologies to link the twin streams of competition and cooperation. The two leading nuclear weapon powers have made some progress in reducing the heaps of weapons of mass destruction.

While making a realistic assessment of the global realities, we must keep in step with the changes. With the predictable certainties of the Cold War gone, international and inter-state relations have become more complicated. There are challenges and also great opportunities for our countries now to get rid of

---

*Speech delivered at the conference of Peace, Asia and South Asia on 27/7/1990.

the shackles of Cold War mindsets that distanced us from our neighbours.

We all are legatees of the colonial economies that inhibited industrial development and impeded friendhip amongst neighbours. In the post-freedom era, we are discovering the benefits of cooperation. The SAARC had decided to reduce the travel and communication tariffs. This has, however, had little impact on economic cooperation. Presently more Indians travel to Singapore and Thailand that to Sri Lanka or Bangladesh. It is time that we learnt from the South-East Asian example, where every member country of the ASEAN has benefited from cooperation. Occasionally they may not agree regarding some security issues but this does not weaken the fabric of their politico-economic cooperation. We now see that the states of Indo-China are drawing closer to the ASEAN making it a larger community of ten nations.

Regrettably, South Asian cooperation continues to languish with an overload of mistrusts. Unless we sympathetically appreciate each other's constraints, we will continue to sink in this quagmire. Frequent meetings at various levels can be helpful to remove the cobwebs of suspicions and mistrusts.

The United Front Government tried to build the needed environment for peace and friendship amongst the neighbours. It succeeded in normalizing relations with Bangladesh and Nepal and withdrew the IPKF from Sri Lanka. Though the renewed fighting between LTTE and the armed forces of Sri Lanka has created anxieties and concerns about another refugee influx, we regard the main issue to be Sri Lanka's internal problem and we do not want to intervene in its internal affairs. Despite these worries our relations with Sri Lanka are better than at any time since 1983 and we hope to build wider economic relations between our two countries in the coming years.

We are ready to open a new forward-looking dialogue with Pakistan and offer hand of genuine good neighbourliness. But the rulers of Pakistan, indeed both the government and the principal opposition parties, mistakenly see in the political trouble in Kashmir an opportunity to wrest the valley. The whole world is aware of how Pakistan is feeding terrorism in Kashmir; thus grossly intervening in our domestic affairs. Even then we are sincere in our desire to normalize relations with it.

What we need in South Asia is to build a cluster of principles around which good neighbourliness could be built on an enduring basis. Our Government tried to do this. We gave solemn assurances to Sri Lanka and Bangladesh that we would not allow the use of Indian Territory against these countries. With Nepal, the open border is, as always a border of friendship, free trade and human beings flowing across it without hindrance. Indeed, Nepal is a text book case of how even temporarily strained relationship can be speedily ended to revive relationships of trust and goodwill on both sides.

Numerous questions could be posed to the ruling elites of Pakistan. Do they really believe that they can get Indian territory by force or subversion? Does sustained hostility with India truly serve the interests of the Pakistan State and its people? Is the policy of abeting terrorism beneficial for the people of Pakistan and is it in conformity with the forces of global change? Will it build a democratic society that people so mush wish for and will restore peace and order in their conflicted provinces; bring about a greater social equilibrium in a highly disjointed society? Or should we not work together to overcome the common problems and join our resources to give the great mass of poor people in our respective countries a better life tomorrow?

The army rulers of Pakistan are asked to address a question that they had avoided all these years: what are the minimum requirements of Pakistan living with India in a peaceful neighbourly co-existence? They must remove from their minds once and for all the doubt they may have nourished all these years against all the evidence to the contrary: that Indians have not accepted Pakistan as a firm political reality. It has been reiterated by many Indians in authority that India wishes Pakistani well, that it is entirely in Indian interest that Pakistan be a stable, united, sovereign democratic state, friendly towards India and other neighbours on terms of mutual benefits.

If Pakistanis come up with a list of their needs for better friendship with India, they are assured that we would look at it with attention and sympathy. Of course, they cannot expect us to give up our territory or modify our secular ethos or allow interventions in our domestic affairs. Nor can growth of any kind of fundamentalism on our soil can be permitted.

We have more than twelve million Muslims living in India. Their contribution in strengthening the India nation state is second to none and the inputs of Islam in our civilization has made us rich and proud. This populace is much larger than the entire population of Pakistan and is the world's second largest Muslim population. Their security and well-being is an integral concern of Indian democracy and secularism. Obviously the promoters of fundamentalism do not care for the welfare of millions of Muslims of India nor for the Muslims of Xiangiang of China or of those in the Central Asian Republics and Afghanistan.

India attaches a lot of importance to SAARC and hopes that it will grow into a viable and vibrant organization of regional cooperation. South Asia, as a geopolitical region, is vastly different from ASEAN. It is a much larger region in area and population and exhibits great symmetries and diversities simultaneously. South-East Asia is a high-growth region while the economy of the ASEAN group is very dynamic in the world of today. Cooperation between India and the ASEAN countries has increased significantly. We have friendly relations with Indonesia, Singapore, Malaysia, Thailand and the Philippines. With each of these countries, our trade and other economic relations are expanding steadily. India's joint ventures in the ASEAN countries are doing well; a positive development is the increasing interest taken by private enterprise in India and the ASEAN countries in expanding economic cooperation.

The South-East Asian region is in the process of rapid integration with the larger region of Asia-Pacific, of which India too is a part. We cannot afford to fall behind global trends and processes. We have to leave the past behind us. We must look at the present as the road to a future of mutual cooperation in peace and friendliness.

23

The Tasks Before SAARC*

The economic environment of the world is undergoing rapid changes, which is affecting, social and political institutions. The World Trade Organization is trying to pattern the world economy to conform with the interests and perceptions of the industrially developed countries. This does not always suit the needs of developing nations. This concept of globalization is seemingly a one-way street that requires us to open our gates for inflow of goods and services, etc., even when it may not be in tune with our needs. To an extent this challenge can be met only if South Asians respond collectively. A united voice of more than one billion people of South Asia with a vast market potential may make an impact.

Axiomatically, the twenty-first century is often projected by the media as the 'Asian Century', wherein South Asia would occupy a mentionable position. Only a determined political will and concerted effort may turn a part of this dream into a reality. Economic cooperation is the main purpose of any regional organization. As it is, trade flows and industrial cooperation in our region are limited. Even collectively, we account for very little in the global trade. This is sad, given the size of our region, its

---

*Keynote address at the inauguration of the SAARC economic conference in New Delhi on 19/11/1996.

potentials, its markets, natural resources and the dramatic growth of entrepreneuring class.

The South Asian Preferential Trade Agreement (SAPTA) has made a modest start since its operationalization in December 1995. All SAARC countries are committed to induct the South Asian Free Trade Area(SAFTA) by the year 2005. At the same time, several studies have shown that SAPTA can induce trade-led growth for this region. India is committed to playing its role keeping in mind the priorities of our neighbours. We need to transform South Asia into a vibrant economic space by optimizing our potentials and opportunities. We may take a leaf from the dramatic successes achieved by other regional bodies in our neighbourhood. We owe it to our people who look to us for such enlightened policies which would raise the region from poverty and backwardness.

As a member of SAARC, India is working to create an environment for the economic uplift of the region as a whole. Preferential trading under SAPTA, for which negotiations were undertaken is an encouraging example. Though initial forward movement was slow but of late it has picked up momentum. While SAPTA has to be the main engine of regional economic cooperation, we must encourage such ideas as would provide added confidence to the inter-governmental bodies.

Travel facilities, tourism, and cheaper telecommunications are needed for creating helpful business environment in the region. Business opportunities do not wait, nor can they be created in the absence of speedy contacts. The SAARC Chamber recommended easing of visa restrictions for bona fide business travellers asking the member States to expedite action to the satisfaction of the business communities. Some Governments did respond helpfully while others did so selectively. In April 1997, I had announced in the Indian Parliament that groups of businessmen and tourists travelling from Pakistan would not need individual visas and businessmen would be granted one-year multi-entry visas.

There are some other aspects needing attention. Sharing of energy is an important issue. All countries in the region suffer from chronic energy shortages caused by paucity of resources. Regional cooperation is bound to help, in this respect, since the enlarged market potential will make the proposition attractive to the investors. Also power management on a larger scale is more economical. Poor business data networking and dissemination constrains economic growth. A great deal remains to be done in the infrastructural sector. There is an abiding feeling that we are not using our resources optimally in a manner which would make economic sense.

As is known, economic growth has a social dimension. With upgradation of education and eradication of illiteracy, the pace of economic growth is bound to touch new heights. The World Trade Organization's debate on the 'social clause' has serious implications for our region. Labour laws, trade union laws, environmental legislation, etc., are of significant relevance for our economies.

Human resource development is an area of vital importance for all of us. We must work our programmes for upliftment of our people. Since there is a dearth of expertise in the region we can share the available talent. We must realize that every member country must attend to the problems confronted by women and the poor to evolve policies for their upliftment and empowerment, that is bound to result in economic development. We may keep in mind that the SAARC has emphasized on partnership between non-governmental organizations to carry forward the social objectives of the Charter.

I suggest that the business Chamber and women's organizations may periodically evaluate the progress and judge for themselves the causes and policies that result in shortfall. Scope of

SAARC activity must expand to offer new opportunities to member countries for networking and cooperative action.

We must appreciate that unless we speedily shed off the heavy burden of divisiveness, the golden dreams of our future will continue to evade us. We have already paid a heavy cost for non-cooperation, and now it is time to say good-bye to these mindsets.

24

The Advantages of Cordial Relations with Neighbours*

The 9th General Elections and the subsequent formation of the UF (United Front) government were significant in many respects. We were witnessing the institutionalization of a coalition culture in the governance of India. The UF Government represented most of the political and regional diversities of India. It was perhaps natural, that, when a coalition of thirteen parties which are seemingly diverse come to power, people may have doubts about its stability. But it is necessary for the discerning and politically aware to appreciate the real message the Indian voter was trying to convey. The mandate was in favour of secular polity and democratic decentralization. It was precisely in accordance with this mandate that the UF coalition was formed. And, despite our diversity, we encountered no difficulty in pursuing clear and coherent objectives. The adoption of the Common Minimum Programme was only the first indicator of the consensus that had emerged in our country on several key policy issues.

The UF Government's CMP (Common Minimum Programme) also set out some of India's important foreign policy objectives. The CMP stated that Non-Alignment would be the cornerstone

*Speech at the luncheon meeting with Academics at Chicago on 29/9/1996.

of our foreign policy and the United Front Government would work to strengthen the movement. Warm and friendly relations with our neighbours received the highest priority, and we used SAARC as an instrument for forging closer relations with them. We took further steps to improve relations with China. We pursued initiatives to participate in or establish linkages with regional arrangements like the Indian Ocean Rim, APEC and the ASEAN. While India had good relations with all countries, it had especially warm relations with the US, Russia and the European Union, among others, and we worked hard to strengthen these relations. We continued the South-South dialogue and promoted open economic interaction with the world. We pledged ourselves to work for universal nuclear disarmament and to retain the nuclear option till this goal was achieved. We also pressed India's case for a permanent seat on the Security Council.

Within these broad objectives, our immediate preoccupation was nuclear disarmament, simply because of the danger, that, if these doomsday weapons exist someday, they might be used to destroy all of us.

Good relations with our neighbours are important since peace, harmony and prosperity are symbiotic. Reform of the UN and the strengthening of international commitment to multilateralism are our priorities because we cannot have global cooperation on peace and development if the UN fails. We also strive to promote economic linkages since we are committed to integrating ourselves into the world economy. Therefore, attracting foreign investment and high technology to India is a high priority.

Why should we place so much importance on our relations with our neighbours, particularly when they are marginal to our trade and investment which was derived mainly from Europe, North America and South East Asia? Our economy is growing much faster than theirs. It could perhaps be argued that we do not need to be excessively concerned about the welfare of our neighbours. That, however, is a simplistic and even a dangerous argument, which we should reject. If India offers more economic opportunities than what is available to people in its neighbourhood, there is great temptation for them to cross borders. Illegal migration into India, which has caused political and social tensions in our border states, would greatly increase. We, therefore, have the same vested interest as, for example, the United States does in enlarging the area of peace and stability around us; we need neighbours who are developing at least as fast as we are. This is why we would place the highest importance on programmes of regional economic cooperation.

There is a further angle to this. In our region, as elsewhere, political problems start with dissatisfaction over the division of a small cake. The disaffected obviously feel that they do not get a fair share of national wealth. Governments, including democratically-elected ones, have an extremely difficult task of balancing the demands of the majority against those of minorities, when both are poor and have equally just claims on limited national resources. The only solution is to increase both national and regional wealth rapidly and equitably. Growth in a region takes place fastest when there is close coordination and cooperation amongst neighbours. Every unhappy ethnic group in our neighbourhood has close links with its counterparts in India, whether they are Tamils in Sri Lanka with Tamils in Tamil Nadu, Chakmas in the Chittagong Hill Tracts with Chakmas in Tripura, or the Nepalese in Bhutan with the Gurkhas in West Bengal. If they are content, there is less unease among their kinsmen in India and this is important for any government in Delhi.

An important aspect of our dealings with our neighbours is to work towards an equitable sharing of natural resources. Throughout, this has always been an extremely sensitive and sometimes contentious matter. The problem is that resources are limited and there are usually equally valid claims from the countries that share them. India is the largest country in the subcontinent. Though willing to go more than half way to accommodate the needs and aspirations of our neighbours, we have to keep in mind that we have the largest number of people dependent on these resources. Therefore, even generosity has to have its limitations. Nevertheless, a viable media is clearly essential; we will not adopt policies that impoverish our neighbours. On the contrary, on more than one occasion, India has travelled more than half way to meet the genuine needs and concerns of its neighbours. In terms of our own interests it will be ruinous for India to be selfish because it would have repercussion for us; refugees and economic migrants in South Asia have really nowhere else to go. We are different nations on our subcontinent, but one people, and in the words of the Bhagavad Gita, *Swajanam hi katham hatva Sukhinah syama madhava* [How can we kill our own people and be happy?]

For exactly the same reasons, namely our collective survival, India is anxious to see genuine progress towards nuclear disarmament. South Asia is surrounded by nuclear weapons, deployed openly or covertly. Globally, the nuclear weapon powers continue to predicate their security, and base their military doctrine, on retaining these weapons, and ensuring no one else gets them. We know that, in negotiations between themselves, they have sharply reduced their holdings, and now humanity can be killed ten times over, instead of thirteen of fifteen times and in all humility, we are all expected to be grateful for this mercy. We are also asked to take comfort that the principal nuclear weapon powers no longer target each other. We ask ourselves on whom do they bestow the favour? If they target no one, and it is not their intention to use them, then why keep nuclear arsenals and make them more lethal?

These questions are answered, of course, by the declared policies of the nuclear weapon powers, in a post-Cold War era, which supposedly make the world a safer place. Throughout the Cold War, the priority for the protaganists remained to deter each other; doctrines for the use of nuclear weapons are never constant, but it was generally believed that they would be used as weapons of last resort against a nuclear-armed enemy. However, no nuclear weapon power rules out a first use of its weapons; this by itself makes the world a much more dangerous place. What is infinitely worse, is that the nuclear weapon powers, finding themselves in a position where, on the one hand, they have to declare that relations between themselves are not being hostile, and on the other, justify their retaining weapons as a means to deter each other, start to define doctrines for their use in regional confrontations with non-nuclear powers. We know that, despite protestations, this use has never been ruled out, but it is now being openly discussed and acknowledged as a possibility.

The world is wriggling on this nuclear hook, from which, if it has to survive, it has to quickly free itself. We are convinced that the highest priority of the international community must be to move towards a genuine peace predicted on the elimination of nuclear weapons. We visualized the Comprehensive Test Ban Treaty as part of a process of nuclear disarmament, leading to the elimination of nuclear weapons within a reasonable timeframe, and immediately ending the testing and qualitative development of nuclear weapons. Unfortunately, the CTBT, as forced through in New York, was neither comprehensive nor a test ban, nor, because of the inequitous provisions for its entry into force, will it ever be a treaty.

The negotiations on the CTBT highlighted the flaws in the UN system. Members of the Conference on Disarmament thought they had a mandate to negotiate a draft by consensus. It turned out that there was an inner core, shielded from the rest, whose members cobbled together a draft to their liking, presenting the rest with a *fait accompli*. When we protested, the Conference on Disarmament, which we were told was sacrosanct, was bypassed with contempt. *Probitas laudatur et alget*, as Juvenal said—praise honesty and ban it.

206

The position taken by India, in the Comprehensive Test Ban Treaty (CTBT) negotiations attracted much international attention. Reactions varied from criticism, to understanding, to appreciation of our policy. The basic issue was that India has and will remain a sincere advocate of complete nuclear disarmament. But we did not and will not accept discriminatory arrangements on the basis of disingenuous arguments, particularly when they have a direct bearing on our national security. A country of one billion people cannot be isolated, least of all when it takes a stand that is valid in terms of any moral or legal norm.

In January 1993, the CWC (Chemical Weapons Convention) was opened for signature. More than 150 countries have signed and 63 countries have ratified this Convention. In keeping with its commitment to becoming an original party to this convention, India too ratified it. We were optimistic that the CWC would enter into force shortly. Yet our optimism was becoming tinged with some concern. The two countries with the largest declared chemical weapons stockpiles had yet to complete their ratification proceedings. While we did not like to doubt their sincerity, it would be inappropriate if narrow concerns overshadowed, and undermined, their stated commitment to the larger role of chemical weapon disarmament.

India and the United States are the world's two largest democracies. Given this inescapable fact, India should attach the highest importance to a friendly and cooperative Indo-US relationship. Our former Prime Minister, PV Narasimha Rao and President Clinton seized a historic opportunity, when in 1994, they agreed to build a 'new partnership' between India and the United States, free of the baggage of the past. Their fresh approach served us well. Indo-US trade, investment, cooperation and broad-based consultations have seen remarkable expansion over the last few years. Both sides have agreed not to allow one or more areas of disagreement to dominate our bilateral relations, or give rise to an acrimonious environment. We should focus on our areas of agreement and try to bridge our differences, always ensuring that differences did not prevent us from moving forward in areas where we can cooperate for our mutual benefit.

Quite apart from economic opportunities, there are more profound reasons for India and the US to come together. There has been a view in the West, and in the United States in particular, that open markets will lead automatically to open political systems and to world peace; yet history would show this hypothesis to be a mere fallacy. Strong economic powers, in Asia and elsewhere, follow their own paths, their own values, their own destinies, and these may not always be peaceful or democratic. It is important, therefore, for democracies everywhere, and for countries like ours, that share a traditional commitment to peace, tolerance and universal human values, to strengthen each other.

25

A New and Cooperative Spirit*

The last decade of the twentieth century saw a profound transformation in the international security environment. The seeds
of the Cold War had already been sown when India became
Independent. In the following decades, the Cold War became
the predominant motif as countries sought to pursue their national security through competing military alliances. India, which
had achieved Independence through a non-violent struggle, that
is unique in history, was determined to protect its Independence
in thought and action. This search for Independence led us, in a
logical manner, to the concept of Non-Alignment. Yet, with the
major powers engaged in an ideological conflict, the Cold War
did cast its shadow on international relations and economic developments. Multilateral institutions set up after the Second World
War to help create a democratic and equitable world order, based
on collective security, were often paralysed by the rivalry between the USA and the former USSR.

The Cold War has ended and we are no longer faced with
two opposing military alliances with their gigantic nuclear arsenals in a state of high alert. The threat perceptions of North
Atlantic Treaty Organization (NATO) and the Warsaw Pact forces
as implacable adversaries, seen through an ideological prism,

*Speech at the United Service Institution of India on 23/1/1997.

are a thing of the past. As profound changes occurred between two former adversaries, there was hope that multilateral institutions like the UN would be revitalised to assume the mantle of collective security. New regional organizations, such as the Organization for Security and Cooperation in Europe (OSCE) the ASEAN, and the Asean Regional Forum have emerged. Existing organizations like NATO are also seeking to redefine their role in trying to tackle existing and future challenges. All this, we hoped, was reflective of a new and cooperative spirit.

It is natural that India's immediate neighbourhood should be a major priority in India's security considerations. A peaceful and constructive environment in our neighbourhood is vital for all of us, if we are to achieve accelerated development for ourselves and for the region as a whole. The South Asian region accounts for roughly one-fourth of all humanity. If this region wants to establish its rightful place in the community of nations, cooperation and mutual goodwill will have to be firmly established as the basis of intra-South Asian relations. Given India's size and situation, it is natural for us to take the initiative in building up confidence and establishing cooperation in all facets of our relationships.

The security of a home lies not only in the bricks and mortar used in its construction but, also upon the goodwill and amity of its inhabitants. India's foreign policy, specially in the context of its neighbourhood, reflects this simple reality.

India has already established that it is ready to go the extra mile to inspire confidence and generate momentum towards a new partnership in South Asia. It is also apparent that we have already achieved substantial success with this approach.

We discussed and implemented new and significant initiatives with Nepal, Bhutan and Bangladesh which steered our relations to higher levels of cooperation. The Treaty, on sharing of Ganga waters, has established a landmark in our relations with Bangladesh, and opened up new vistas of constructive collaboration in all areas of our interaction. It is a matter of pride that this Treaty was welcomed, not only in India and Bangladesh, but the world over, and is a clear demonstration of what can be achieved with sincerity and a sense of purpose. In time we expected the entire eastern region of the subcontinent, including Nepal, Bhutan, Bangladesh and India to see a surge of development through cooperation in the areas of transport, energy development, water management, etc.

Likewise, with Sri Lanka, we expressed our desire to assist, without being intrusive, in an early settlement of the conflict in that country. Such an outcome would have beneficial results for India and the entire region. We would like the Palk Straits to become a gateway for peaceful commerce and communication among our people. We dreamt of once again making the maritime frontier, which India and Sri Lanka share, an area of peace, and then take up collaborative ventures for advanced research on ocean resources. Situated as we both are at the centre of the Indian Ocean, our maritime interests are close and intertwined. Together with Maldives, our partner in the SAARC, we wanted to explore possibilities to turn this region into a prosperous growth area. Our friendship also provides an anchor for the security and prosperity of the Indian Ocean region.

With regard to Pakistan, we gave them an offer for a dialogue between the two countries soon after our Government took office. Even while we were awaiting Pakistan's response, we were taking unilateral steps to improve the relationship at the people-to-people level. We were also trying to preserve a positive atmosphere, by avoiding polemic, and ignoring the occasional hostile rhetoric from across the border.

In this period of significant change, where we are trying to transform the politico-economic face of our region, the concept of security has to be viewed afresh. Security can no longer be visualised in narrow military terms. It calls for inter-dependence among all countries in the world, to tackle non-conventional and non-military threats arising out of international terrorism, narcotics, ethnic conflicts, fundamentalism, environmental pollution, natural disasters, etc., all of which impinge upon the over-all security of nations. A redefinition of old concepts requires new thinking and fresh approaches, if we are to successfully deal with the challenges posed by an uncertain future. More so, there is a growing realization that what is needed is a collective approach, based upon cooperation rather than competition and confrontation.

Nowhere is this more valid than in the area of nuclear disarmament. We are told that the US and the Russian Federation no longer target their missiles at each other. Yet, there is a reluctance to accept the notion that elimination of nuclear weapons is the only practical and lasting way to deal with the scourge of nuclear proliferation, as well as to enhance global security. The acceptance of the philosophy of interdependence and collective security has been successful in dealing with biological and chemical weapons, and we see no reason why it cannot be used to rid the world of the nuclear shadow.

When the CTBT was concluded after two and a half years of intensive negotiations, it was a source of great disappointment to us that India, which had made the first call for ending nuclear testing in 1954, was unable to subscribe to the Treaty because of its fundamental shortcomings. The CTBT, as it emerged, was no longer linked to the process of nuclear disarmament. It only prohibited nuclear testing and therefore, could not be described as a comprehensive treaty that would ban all kinds of nuclear testing whether based on explosions or other techniques.

We were not simplistic enough to call for nuclear disarmament to be achieved overnight. Yet, we are also realistic enough to believe that the end of the Cold War offered us a unique opportunity to demonstrate our commitment to the goal of a world free of nuclear weapons. This commitment should be translated into reality by commencing negotiations on a Nuclear

Weapons Convention that would not only prohibit the development, deployment, production, stockpiling and transfer of nuclear weapons but also provide for their elimination within an agreed timeframe. It was heartening to note that there is a growing interest in discussing these issues, particularly the technical aspects relating to verification. These deliberations, being undertaken by Non-government Organizations, are welcome.

Confidence Building Measures were another important aspect of international security and needed to be strengthened in order to reduce mistrust and allay apprehensions. These measures took different forms. To begin with, political declarations were important but in the long run, these were not enough. Means of communication and dialogue had to be established in order to substantiate the political declarations. This implies a degree of transparency. Participation in global efforts like the UN Arms Register and regional initiatives about military information sharing, cooperation in region specific issues such as maritime security were potential areas for consideration. Once the channels of communication were established and confidence had been built up, discussions on regional defence issues were feasible.

These processes that had been identified are not new. We have seen that Confidence Building Measures were introduced and practised in Europe during the last two decades. However, there is one fundamental difference. In the post-Cold War world, these Confidence Building Measures had to be negotiated not among two alliances but among sovereign nations in a cooperative spirit. Every country brings its own legitimate concerns to the negotiating table which need to be addressed adequately. Unlike during the Cold War when such measures were seen in a bi-polar context, confidence building now has to be seen as an exercise to create a pluralistic security order.

My government did a lot of work for instituting CBMs with both Pakistan and China. In fact, this was carried significantly forward in case of China when their President visited us.

213

Such developments at a regional level do not diminish the emphasis on globalization which has been a cornerstone of India's foreign policy. They complement the global approach in a manner that has become feasible now, with the end of the Cold War. But security concerns or threats have not altogether disappeared. But we now have more instruments and institutions available to us in order to deal with these concerns in a manner consistent with the traditional principles of the Indian foreign policy. Perhaps, it is easier for India to engage in such a dialogue with its various interlocutors compared to some other countries which were members of military alliances during the Cold War. For them, a post-Cold War period requires major shifts in thinking. For us, it reflects a new opportunity to strengthen ties with our immediate neighbours.

26

The Ganga Water's Treaty with Bangladesh*

The first visit of the former Bangladesh Prime Minister, Sheikh Hasina, to India since she assumed office, came as the culmination of a series of exchanges initiated shortly after the United Front government took office. This period of intense interaction had placed our relations on an entirely new footing. Progress was being made on all issues in our bilateral relations. The prominent issue in our bilateral ties, over the last two decades has been the issue of sharing of Ganga waters of Farakka, which was resolved when the Prime Ministers of India and Bangladesh signed a new treaty on the sharing of the Ganga water. This Treaty was a landmark in our bilateral relations. It protected the interests of India and at the same time helped Bangladesh by providing it an adequate share of the Ganga water.

According to the Treaty, sharing of Ganga water at Farakka between India and Bangladesh would be on the basis of a formula whose key merit was that it shared available waters on a fair and equitable basis. The formula also took into account the basic requirements and minimum needs of both sides. There-

---

*Suo Moto statement delivered in the Rajya Sabha on 12/12/1996 on the visit of Prime Minister of the People's Republic of Bangladesh to India and the signing of the Treaty of sharing of Ganga water at Farakka.

fore, it was proposed that during the critical period within the lean season, i.e. from March 1 to May 10, India and Bangladesh each would receive a guaranteed flow of 35,000 cusecs of water in an alternative sequence of three 10-day periods each. This is aimed at meeting the fundamental requirements of both our countries through a just and reasonable sharing of the burden of shortage. The Treaty also has the merit of being a long-term arrangement combined with scope for reviews at shorter intervals to study the impact of the sharing formula and to make needed adjustments. While the Treaty is valid for 30 years and renewable on mutual consent, there is a provision of mandatory reviews at the end of 5 years and even earlier, i.e., after 2 years with provisions for making adjustments as required. Depending on a fresh understanding reached after the review stage, Bangladesh would continue to receive 90 per cent of its share in accordance with the new formula. We could thus avoid a situation where there is no agreement on the sharing of the Ganga water between India and Bangladesh.

The signing of the Treaty between India and Bangladesh was a fitting tribute to the special quality of our relations. Indo-Bangladesh cooperation was based on a history of shared sacrifices, sanctified with the blood of the martyrs who laid down their lives in 1971. It was entirely appropriate that this Treaty came on the eve of the twenty-fifth anniversary of the liberation of Bangladesh, which was a momentous landmark in the history of our subcontinent. With the signing of this Treaty, we looked forward to a new era in Indo-Bangladesh relations. This new relationship proved to be of immense benefit to India, in the long-term, in all areas of bilateral relations including security, trade and other areas. With the removal of what had been a constant irritant in bilateral ties, we could look forward to an entirely new phase of cooperation. We had already taken initiatives in the commercial sphere by extending tariff concessions to Bangladesh on a range of products of export interest to them.

We proposed to extend commercial credits of Rs 100 crore to enhance trade relations further. We were working together with Bangladesh to ensure appropriate development and security in our entire eastern region.

It would be appropriate also at this stage to place on record our appreciation of the very constructive role played by the then Chief Minister of West Bengal and his cabinet colleagues in bringing about an improved atmosphere in which the Treaty between India and Bangladesh could become possible. My appreciation are also due to the Ministries of Water Resources and Surface Transport for their invaluable support in this endeavour.

Both India and Bangladesh have cooperated extensively in the regional fora such as SAARC and it was our endeavour to take this cooperation forward so that a new and more constructive framework of relationships could be built up in our subcontinent to the mutual benefit of the people of all countries.

27

Developments in Sino-Indian Relations*

The visit of President Jiang Zemin in 1996 was the first of its kind by a President of the People's Republic of China to India. This state visit from 28 November 1996 to 1 December 1996, was a part of an ongoing dialogue at the highest level initiated with the visit of former Prime Minister Rajiv Gandhi to China in 1988. Our former President, R. Venkataraman, and former Prime Minister, PV Narasimha Rao, had also visited China. We had already received Premier Li Peng and other high-ranking Chinese leaders in India. The Parliaments of the two countries have always maintained contacts, with the visits of the Honourable Speaker of the Lok Sabha and the Honourable Deputy Chairman of the Rajya Sabha to China and their Chinese counterparts to India. These high-level exchanges permitted us to discuss, in a constructive manner, all relevant issues in our bilateral relations.

Indo-China relations has acquired maturity and substance. While continuing to address outstanding issues, including the boundary question, we seek to expand mutually beneficial co-operation in all areas. This policy, pursued over the last several

---

*Suo Moto statement delivered in both houses of Parliament on 5/12/1996 on the occasion of the visit of the President of the People's Republic of China.

operation in all areas. This policy, pursued over the last several years, reflects the consensus in the Parliament which transcended party lines.

Both sides expressed their satisfaction with the outcome of the visit, which afforded us an opportunity to assess the current state of relations as well as prospects for our relationship in the future. During their talks, the then Indian Prime Minister Mr Deve Gowda and President Jiang agreed that India and China should work towards a constructive and cooperative relationship, while continuing to address outstanding differences. They also shared the assessment that friendly and good neighbourly relations between India and China served the fundamental interests of the two peoples.

A significant outcome of the visit was the signing of the Agreement on Confidence Building Measures in the Military Field along the Line of Actual Control on the Indo-China border areas. This agreement was built on the foundation of the agreement on the maintenance of peace and tranquility along the Line of Actual Control in the Indo-China Border Areas, signed in September 1993 during the visit of the then Prime Minister, PV Narasimha Rao, to China. The Agreement of 1993 committed the two countries to respect the Line of Actual Control (LAC) and take a series of steps to clarify the LAC, devise additional Confidence Building Measures (CBMs) and move towards force reduction in border areas. These Agreements on CBMs stipulated that neither side shall use its military capability against the other side. It laid down some important guiding principles for reduction or limitation of identified categories of military forces and armaments, to mutually agreed ceilings within mutually agreed geographical zones along the LAC. The extent of the geographical zones as well as the ceilings were to be decided in subsequent negotiations between the Joint Working Group and the Expert Group. The agreement also provided for a number of important CBMs, which helped in preserving peace and tranquility in border areas. The two sides also agreed to accelerate the process of the clarification of the entire LAC, fecilitated through an exchange of maps.

The agreement on CBMs represented a major step forward in our efforts to ensure that the Indo-China border areas remained peaceful. We believed that the full implementation of the two agreements would help in advancing our agenda of developing an institutionalized framework for consultations, co-operation and maintenance of peace and tranquility in border areas, and, for moving towards forced reduction of military presence, along the Indo-China LAC in a manner which fully safeguards our national security interests.

During the discussions between former Prime Minister Deve Gowda and the Chinese President Jiang Zemin, the two sides agreed to continue their efforts to seek a fair, reasonable and mutually acceptable settlement of the boundary question. This understanding was reflected in the agreement on CBMs. Agreements, like the one made in 1993, made due provision for the fact that its implementation would be without prejudice to the respective positions of India and China on the boundary question.

During the discussions, the two sides agreed to impart a much greater economic and technological content to their relationship. It was agreed that the next meeting of the Joint Economic Group, co-chaired by the Chinese Minister for Foreign Trade and Economic Cooperation and myself was to be held in the first quarter of 1997 to work for a significant expansion of economic cooperation and trade between India and China. The Indo-China sub-group on Science and Technology would also meet to look at greater opportunities for enhancing functional cooperation between the two countries.

Apart from the agreement on CBMs, three other agreements were signed. These agreements were related to the maintenance of our consular establishment in Hong Kong after it reverted to the Chinese sovereignty on 1 July 1997, cooperation in combating illicit drug trafficking and other major crimes, and maritime transport. These agreements contributed to the development of an institutionalized framework for inter-State and people-to-people contacts between India and China.

Useful exchange of views on regional and international issues, including recent developments in Afghanistan and Myanmar were carried out. Prospects of cooperation in Central Asia were also discussed. We briefed the Chinese President on our efforts to improve relations with all countries of South Asia. We also exchanged views on the reform of the UN system, including the question of giving adequate representation to the Non-Aligned and other developing countries in the UN organs. We pointed out that any objective criteria for the restructuring of the UN Security Council would provide for India's inclusion in the expanded Security Council as a permanent member. The two sides agreed that the dialogue on regional and international issues and cooperation in international fora were mutually beneficial and must be expanded.

In our discussions with the Chinese President and the Vice-Premier and Foreign Minister, we conveyed our concerns regarding Chinese sales of missiles and other weapons to Pakistan and their assistance to Pakistan's nuclear programme. It was also conveyed to the Chinese President that Sikkim was an integral part of India and that we would expect early Chinese recognition of this reality. The importance of paying adequate attention to each other's concerns on vital issues affecting are respective unities, territorial integrities and security, was underlined. We proposed to continue our dialogue with China on these important issues.

The visit of the Chinese President to India represented a significant step forward in the process of steady improvement of our relations with our largest neighbour, China. It provided the two countries an opportunity to assess the current state of relationship at the highest level and also move towards a long-term basis for a cooperative and constructive relationship. While reiterating their determination to resolve the boundary question in a fair, reasonable and mutually acceptable manner, the two sides agreed, in the interim, on concrete measures to ensure that peace and tranquility were maintained. The visit was utilized to convey to the Chinese side our concerns on some vital issues affecting the unity, territorial integrity and security of India.

28

The Afghan Situation in 1996*

The developments in Afghanistan in 1996 attracted worldwide attention and evoked deep concerns. The fall of Kabul to the Taliban forces was a turning point. It led to the brutal murder of former President Najibullah and his brother. It was all the more shocking because they were under the charge of the UN, which was honour bound to protect them. The Government of India had expressed its deep revulsion at this tragic development.

The pursuit of obscurantist doctrines by the Taliban leadership and the consequent denial of human rights, especially the rights of women, was extensively condemned. The implications of these events were assessed, especially the risk of an adverse impact on India's security. We continued to carefully follow the developments in Afghanistan very closely and evaluated the implications for us.

The situation in Afghanistan was in a state of flux. The opposing parties facing each other in battle were the Taliban and the forces of the Supreme Council for the Defence of Afghanistan (SCDA), comprising the forces of General Rashid Dostum and of Hizb-e-Wahdat leader Karim Khalili. The fronts in the vicinity of Kabul and in the western part of Afghanistan witnessed sporadic activity. After a period of tranquility, there were

---

*Suo Moto statement delivered in both houses of Parliament, New Delhi.

reports of renewed heavy fighting north of Kabul. The onset of winter increased the difficulties of the people, enhancing their need for humanitarian assistance.

We maintained contact with the legitimate Afghan Government led by President Rabbani. Though we had to withdraw our Embassy on 27 September 1996, the Afghan Embassy continued to function in Delhi. President Rabbani met our Prime Minister during his visit to Rome for the Food Summit. We had also sent a delegation led by Secretary (East) in the Ministry of External Affairs to Mazar-e-Sharif to meet General Rashid Dostum. We were in contact with countries that took interest in the Afghan situation. We were keen to assist in restoration of peace and tranquility there.

Subsequently, the UN Secretary General convened a meeting of senior officials and experts from 19 countries, who had some knowledge about Afghanistan. India was invited and we participated in the meeting. India was also invited to take part in an international forum sponsored by UN to provide assistance to Afghanistan.

The significant elements of our position on the Afghanistan situation were:

- India fully supported the unity, independence, territorial integrity and sovereignty of Afghanistan. These were essential for the well-being of the Afghan people and, given Afghanistan's strategic location, for the peace and stability of the entire region.
- Cessation of foreign interference in Afghanistan remains an essential pre-requisite for the resolution of the situation.
- We fully supported the efforts of the UNSG and its special representative in bringing peace to Afghanistan. India was prepared to play its full part in supporting the efforts of the UN special Mission to Afghanistan.
- The cessation of violence and armed hostilities and the de-

militarization of Afghanistan would provide the right conditions to pursue a democratic political process. We supported all the measures in this respect.

• The cessation of arms supply to Afghanistan was necessary. The effective implementation of this idea had to be carefully worked out.

• The growth in drug trafficking and terrorism, which was a result of conflict in Afghanistan, were matters of deep concern to us and rest of the world.

We are greatly disturbed and distressed at the denial of human rights, especially those of the women, in Afghanistan. We entirely support the denunciation of these practices contained in the UN Security Council Resolution 1076. The Resolution 'denounces the discrimination against girls and women and other violations of human rights and international humanitarian law in Afghanistan, and notes with deep concern possible repercussions on international relief and reconstruction programmes in Afghanistan'. In this context, we reiterated our condemnation of the brutal and abhorrent murder of former President Najibullah and his brother.

Even during uncertain conditions, we continued to offer humanitarian assistance to Afghanistan in the form of medicines, foodstuff and clothing. We also conducted a month-long camp in Kabul in August-September, 1996, for fitting artificial limbs on persons who had lost their limbs, mostly on account of land mines. Over 1100 such limbs were fitted in the camp.

We had seen reliable reports in the international media that the Taliban were training terrorists and arming the Harkat-Ul-Ansar. It was reported that at these training camps, not only Pakistani but young soldiers of other nationalities were being trained to carry out terrorist activities in Kashmir. The Government of India and the people of our country continued to sustain their vigil and were taking all necessary steps to safeguard the country's security.

Our interaction with Afghanistan was constructive and positive. It was not directed at any other country. Its purpose was to assist in bringing peace and stability to a country with which we have civilizational affinities and are bound by ties of brotherhood, friendship and cooperation.

29

Indo-Nepal Cooperation in a Changing World*

There is a long tradition in history of intellectuals and politicians working in tandem for common purposes. Intellectuals are not ivory tower recluses, cut off from the travails of the human condition. The true intellectual is, on the contrary, the conscience keeper of the society and, thus, the guide of those on whom the people have entrusted the governance of the nation. On the other hand,politicians are not merely the practitioners of realpolitik, unconcerned with the grand vision or great ideas of remoulding societies and restructuring inter-State relations. It is the sacred duty of both intellectuals and politicians on both sides of our common free borders, to bring their collective energies, their sense of history, their power of analysis, their understanding of global changes and, above all, their idealism and vision, to the refashioning of Indo-Nepal relations.

The Indo-Nepal relationship is not merely historic; it is unique. This, for me, is the basic, fundamental premise. Our ties cannot be compared with any other, in our region or outside it. They are so ancient that they surpass the memory of man. If we take the objective realities into account, nothing divides us; and there

---

*Speech delivered at the Nepal Council of World Affairs on 6/8/1990.

are innumerable bonds that unite us. Goods and human population have moved across the 1,700 kilometers of the border between us in a continuing, unhindered stream. We share more than what we care to make ourselves realize. Viewed in this perspective, nothing could have been more unnatural, more against the dictates of geography and the tide of history and more against the will of our people than the aberration in Indo-Nepal relations that prevailed in early 1990s. Therefore, the first task for both our Governments was to restore our old time-tested relationship.

The visit of Prime Minister Krishna Prasad Bhattarai to India in 1990 provided the most appropriate opportunity for fully normalizing our relations. The Joint Communique of 10 June, 1990 signed by our two Prime Ministers was precisely designed to perform this task. Since then, things moved fast. All the commitments on the Indian side were fulfilled. Nepal has also fulfilled most of its commitments.

Our experience however, taught us both something of value. And it is that we must treat treaties as close as ours with utmost care. Moreover, it is necessary to appreciate each other's genuine concerns in the proper spirit and accommodate them as far as possible. Without this approach, no relationship, however time-tested, can endure itself. In future, we must not allow the past to repeat itself.

The world talks of open borders and of closer interaction between people. India and Nepal have shared all this for ages. Should we not make sure that we retain our role as a model, not only for South Asia, but also for the whole world?

Today, political landscapes the world over are changing. Divided people are being united; long-standing barriers are being pulled down, not by the might of the State power but by the assertion of the will of the people. Old fears are being discarded and new hopes being reborn—hopes of working and growing together, of banishing all wars, except the war on scarcity. For decades, the foreign policies and even the domestic policies of many developing countries were deeply affected by the Cold War. Now that the Cold War chapter has been formally closed, we in the developing countries have the opportunity of developing our economies and cooperating with each other, unhindered by outside interference and influences.

We have to reappraise not only our position in the world, but also our linkages with the new configurations of power that are emerging in the West. We have to understand the deeper directions and the meaning of the global changes that are taking place so that we can keep in step with them without losing our national moorings. There are great opportunities for us. At the same time, the world has become much more complicated and our economic problems are even more intertwined now with what goes on in the mainstream of the world economy. We must develop a combined capability of identifying opportunities and taking advantage of them and also coping with the challenges that the rapidly changing world is posing, and avoiding the dangers and the pitfalls that accompany it.

One of the clearly discernible trends of global change has been the assertion of fundamental democratic urges by different ethnic groups—their powerful desire to move in the direction of multi-party systems of governance, and to exercise fundamental freedoms and basic human rights. Eastern Europe has been the witness to the triumph of these basic urges and values. What happened in Eastern Europe had its impact on other parts of the world also.

Closer home, the magnificent success of the mass movement in Nepal for the restoration of multi-party democracy in 1990 was one of the happiest and most brilliant successes of this democratic wave. However, what happened in Nepal was not the import of democratic values from outside, but the assertion of its own old tradition and the success of democratic experiments which were rudely shaken twice during the last fifty years.

Through their remarkable tenacity the people of Nepal are well on their way to establish a new democratic order. Thereby, one more bond, that of shared democratic values, was added to the innumerable ties that already link Nepal and India.

For us, human rights have not merely been an aspect of a nation state's relationship with its people, but also a deep human concern, that is felt both by the rulers and the ruled. In some of our ancient polities it was in fact the ruled who were the real rulers.

Human rights, above all, demand a commitment to social justice. No democratic system can be sustained without social justice. Without it, the cleavages in a nation will grow even deeper and become unbridgeable. Lord Buddha—whose teachings both India and Nepal share as a precious heritage—taught us, above all, the need for compassion for the weak and the downtrodden. We do not need learned lectures on the need for social justice from foreign experts. All that we have to do is to remember the message of that Prince of Peace.

Recent developments have exposed the grave limitations of the pursuit of security only through narrow military means. The real threat to our domestic social order, as well as to the international order, today stems from the non-military threats to security—the degradation of the environment; the distortions which excessive military expenditure have introduced in the global economy and the way they are crippling the national economies of major military spenders and perpetuating inequality among nations and, above all, the denial of social justice within nations is astounding.

The success of the democratic movement imposed upon Nepal the momentous task of drafting its new democratic constitution. Here, it is worthwhile remembering that democracy does not begin and end with the right to vote, that a modern constitution is not merely designed to guarantee formal democratic rights, but also is an instrument for guaranteeing social justice and for

230

bringing about social transformation. It is also important, through the constitution-making process, to build strong institutions which derive their powers from the people's representatives, and to ensure that they are consciously and continuously protected and kept strong and vibrant. I knew that those who were entrusted with the task of drafting Nepal's constitution were knowledgeable and more acutely aware of their historic responsibility than any outside constitutional adviser can ever claim to be.

An important feature of the changes in Nepal and in other parts of the world in the begining of the 1990s was sometimes described as the collapse of ideology. But this is only a limited peripheral judgment. In reality, what happened was that the old frame of reference was now missing. The totalitarian and excessively regulated form in which socialism has been practised in Eastern Europe and in many other countries of the world disintegrated under the weight of its own contradictions. But all societies require an ideology in the deeper and broader sense of the term. King Ashoka, who is, again, our great common heritage, tried to define religion in one of the stone pillars that he erected for the education of his people. He said: Religion is that which holds the world together.

We, thus, always need a system of values, to hold the society together, and in the modern era, to conduct inter-State relations. The most important aspect of the Socialist ideology, is its commitment to social justice. In fact, this aspect has been effectively hijacked by the so-called capitalist societies which have much greater resources at their disposal to underwrite social welfare schemes. Social welfare schemes have become the hallmark of Western civilization and attempts are afoot to make them increasingly cost-effective.

Human rights today are threatened not only by what the State can do to its people but also by the worldwide rise of terrorism, religious fundamentalism and other forms of extremism—often encouraged and abetted by assistance from outside.

The latter aspect goes against all canons of conducting mutually fruitful inter-State relations and is proving an effective barrier to bilateral and regional cooperation.

The technological revolution is by far the most potent new factor operating in the world today. It has led to the integration of markets and changed the pattern of global production, consumption and trade. It has made nations more interdependent than ever before, and issues more interrelated and complex. The implications of economic policies of major powers today travel beyond their national frontiers and decisively influence the growth and prosperity of other countries. This has made cooperation inevitable and arbitrary; unilateral actions not only disrupt growth and stability but are also counterproductive. The revolution in information technology has substantially altered the methods and styles of managing economies, governing states and even conducting inter-State relations. The new revolution can be harnessed for the service of liberty and freedom and for bringing growth and prosperity. It is no longer necessary for nations to go through all the stages of growth, about which so much was written in the early post-Cold War period, before reaching the so-called take-off stage. Technology has made possible the leapfrogging of stages of growth.

At the same time, monopoly over the new and emerging technologies has emerged as the single most important factor, which is further widening the economic gap between the developed and developing countries. This is also being used by the technologically-advanced countries for perpetuating their privileged position in the international power structure. This they are seeking to do by denying developing countries access to these technologies by adopting restrictive business practices, by erecting new discriminatory regimes with regard to dual-purpose technologies and by seeking to establish a regime for the protection of intellectual property rights.

Foreign policy decisions today are no longer merely political in nature. Economic interest is now coming to play a crucial role in this process. The supreme necessity of international cooperation in the field of conserving our environment is an example of how scientific and technological factors play a crucial role in international relations.

The problem of the protection of environment has become one of the most important global issues today. This task cannot now be left to the judgement of individual nation states alone, the need to reach a 'global compact' has become essential. But, here too, we saw, as in the case of the Montreal Convention on the Control of Production of Chlorofluro Carbons (CFC) and different suggestions to cope with the problem of Greenhouse Effect, that a solution to this problem was being sought at the cost of the developing world. They were being obliged to make disproportionate sacrifices. As a result, there is a danger of the freezing of their development at existing levels.

In discussions on this crucial subject, the endeavour of my government was that Nepal and India work jointly, along with other developing countries, to ensure that the approach adopted for dealing with this problem is not merely regulatory but a comprehensive one; that the main burden for imposing restrictions on production and consumption of substances which pose a threat to the environment is borne by those who have been mainly responsible for environmental degradation and that the developing countries are granted access to environmentally benign technologies and given the resources to be able to do so.

A major impact of the technological revolution has been the gradual erosion of the concept of nation state as we have known it. In the present integrated global economic system, nation states are being increasingly called upon to surrender their sovereignty and are doing so even without being conscious of it. In order to maintain the competitiveness of their economies, they are also moving in the direction of the integration of markets. This has given a big fillip to regional cooperation, particularly among industrialized countries. This development is no unmixed blessing for developing countries. Countries outside these groupings, particularly the developing countries, are fearing discrimination and even worse.

There are strong reasons to believe that the system that is emerging in Western Europe is going to be based on the old nineteenth century concept of balance of power and is hegemonic, both in design and purpose. I have already referred to the discriminatory, partial and ad hoc trade and technology regimes that are being sought to be put in place. In the security field, deterrence is now being sought by Western countries not against each other but against imagined threats from outside countries, which means developing countries. To cite a historical example of our experience, it seems that the East India Company is remerging with a new global face. Given these circumstances, Nepal and India can no longer afford to live in the past. We have to think of our new responsibilities in the changing world, which we can discharge only by forging new relationship and devising new methods of cooperation. Neither of us can now afford to remain frightened by imaginary ghosts so far as our mutual cooperation is concerned. The Joint Communique issued by our two Prime Ministers in 1990 was a broad indication of the areas in which possibilities of such cooperation exist. Together, we should seek to deal with the problems of the environment and the protection of our common ecology. Harnessing of the waters of the common rivers will obviously play a very important role in controlling the degradation of the environment, apart from bringing a host of other positive benefits of an unprecedented dimension. How long can we avoid doing something which we must inevitably do?

The National Front Government was committed to Nepal's industrialization and in building a self-reliant economy for it. This government tried to ensure the flow of financial resources into Nepal at a much higher level, and provide uninhibited entry of the Nepalese products into the Indian markets.

With Nepal, forging new links and building a comprehensive framework of cooperation brooks no delay. Nepal stands poised on the threshold of a promising new democratic era. The Nepalese people are busy establishing a system which will enable them to harness their creative energies for seeking a better life for themselves and for playing their rightful role in the comity of nations. True to its historic tradition, India has always extended its arm of friendship and cooperation to Nepal.

30

Pakistan's Intervention in Kashmir—I*

I visited New York from 22 to 26 April 1990 in order to participate in the Special Session of the UN General Assembly devoted to International Economic Cooperation and in the Non-Aligned Foreign Ministers' meeting connected with this Special Session. I had extensive discussions with my counterparts from a large number of countries during my stay in New York.

The background to the meeting with Pakistan's Foreign Minister were the tensions and aberrations created in Indo-Pak relations due to Pakistan's involvement in generating extremism and violence in Jammu and Kashmir. Despite Pakistan's obdurate attitude on this issue, the Government of India had kept lines of communication open with authorities in Pakistan to avoid confrontation and to revive the process of normalization and stability in Indo-Pak relations.

In conformity with India's commitment to conduct relations with Pakistan in the spirit of bilateralism inherent in the Simla Agreement, I took advantage of my visit to New York to have a detailed exchange of views with the Foreign Minister of Pakistan, Sahabzada Yakub Khan on 25 April 1990. During the course of this meeting, I reiterated that Pakistan's continued intervention in Jammu and Kashmir and its support and encouragement

*Reply made in the Rajya Sabha on 2/5/1990.

236

to terrorism was not conducive to maintenance of peace in our region and that such an approach would be detrimental to Indo-Pak relations. I stressed that adventurist brinkmanship on the part of Pakistan, in relation to Jammu and Kashmir, could generate unpredictable events which might become uncontrollable.

I told him that since our last meeting, instead of listening to my advice for restraint, Pakistan had stepped up interventionist actions in Punjab and Kashmir through training and supply of arms to subversive elements and by incitement to violence. Belligerent and inflammatory rhetoric exhorting people to resort to arms was being indulged in at very responsible political levels. Calls for a 'Thousand Years War' and for *Jehad* were being issued from the same quarters. Special Kashmir Funds for supporting insurgency had been created. Government-sponsored media campaign had increased manifold. Advertisements were appearing in the press asking for recruits for *Jehad*. *Fatehas* were being read in mosques and in the Parliament for the terrorists. A Pakistani citizen sitting in the USA was owning up responsibilities for kidnappings and killings conducted in India, and also openly asking his so-called followers to assassinate the Indian Prime Minister and the Leader of the Opposition. Reports had appeared in the Pakistani press stating that the Pakistan government had sought the assistance of the United States government for facilitating the mission of this Pakistani citizen in the United States. Efforts were being made to send Pakistani citizens across the Line of Actual Control. There had already been three recorded instances of Pakistani citizens crossing the Line of Actual Control.

I impressed upon the Pakistan's Foreign Minister that if Pakistan indeed sought peace and friendship, it must take tangible and credible measures to withdraw support from terrorism and desist from intervention in our internal affairs. Concrete evidence of this happening alone would provide the point of departure for building up friendly relations with Pakistan.

Pakistan's Foreign Minister denied that Pakistan was encouraging subversion and terrorism in India and reiterated Pakistan's well-known position regarding Kashmir and 'self-determination'. I countered this by telling Sahabzada Yakub Khan that Pakistan could not gloss over the facts and that it was still not too late for Pakistan to withdraw from the brinkmanship.

During the course of the discussion, Pakistan's Foreign Minister made the patently propagandist suggestion that we invite the United Nations or an outside agency to confirm the factual situation on the ground and to provide a 'neutral surveillance mechanism'. I rejected this suggestion and reminded him that both countries had consciously agreed on the irrelevance and redundancy of the third party involvement in bilateral relations in the Simla Agreement long ago. I also pointed out that this suggestion was neither helpful nor feasible. He should know that no international agency could effectively monitor clandestine assistance to terrorists. There was no alternative to Pakistan taking appropriate and credible measures in order to create confidence and demonstrate its seriousness about improving relations with India.

At the end of the talks, similarly-worded press statements were made:

The two Foreign Ministers had a frank, business like and useful exchange of views. Both sides agreed that tension should be reduced and confrontations avoided.

For this purpose, it was agreed that:

(a) The Director General of Military Operations of India and Pakistan should remain in touch with each other.
(b) Both sides should exercise restraint.
(c) Channels of communications should be kept open at all levels.

My bilateral talks with the Pakistan's Foreign Minister were useful in that they offered me the opportunity to impress upon the Pakistan's Foreign Minister the dangers inherent in their policy of supporting terrorism and subversion in India and the need on their part to take urgent remedial action. We were watching the situation carefully. We had kept communication channels open and if Pakistan gave concrete evidence on the ground of applying restraint, it would pave the way for normalization and improvement of our bilateral relations.

India was wedded to peace. However, the Government of India will never tolerate infringements on its sovereignty and territorial integrity.

31

Pakistan's Intervention in Kashmir—II*

There is a national consensus on the basic postulates of India's foreign policy. These were articulated during the course of our freedom struggle and enunciated by no less a person than Pandit Jawaharlal Nehru himself. There is also a global change taking place and our policies must respond to it. While we must look and react globally, we attach great importance to harmonious relationships amongst South Asians. This is contrary to Pakistan's ongoing belligerence. The end of the Cold War now denies it the support it used to get before. By pursuing an outmoded policy of belligerence Pakistan is missing a great opportunity of peace and friendship with India. If Pakistan wishes for friendship and normalization of relations, we will heartily welcome it. India is ever willing for a bilateral dialogue to establish constructive and cooperative relationships.

We believe in the letter and spirit of the Simla Agreement and are committed to settle all differences peacefully through bilateral negotiations. The Simla Agreement had clearly laid down that all differences would be resolved bilaterally through negotiations. I had, in this spirit, readily accepted Pakistan's suggestion for talks. I wished to impress upon the Government of

---

*Reply made in Rajya Sabha on 3/5/1990.

Pakistan the inherent dangers in their policy of brinkmanship that they continue to follow.

Several countries appealed for reduction of tensions in Indo-Pak relations and for avoidance of confrontations. To view these well meaning appeals as pressures would be incorrect and out of context. We never accepted pressures from any side. This is the legacy of our foreign policy. We ourselves believe that tensions and confrontations are not in the interest of the people of the two countries and are not conducive to peace and stability in the region. According to media reports, *Mohtarma* Benazir Bhutto, the then Prime Minister of Pakistan had said that she was ready to meet our Prime Minister for a dialogue to resolve differences over Kashmir. This conformed with what we had always sought, i.e. bilateral discussions at all levels to sort out contentious issues between the two neighbour countries. Difficulties emanated from the preconditions that Pakistan's Prime Minister had proposed for such a dialogue and from Pakistan's continued support to subversion and terrorism in Punjab and Jammu and Kashmir. She had asked for observance of the outdated UN Resolutions. She also referred to 'troop deployment and neutral mechanism' to verify allegations and counter allegations from both sides. These statements were similar to what Sahabzada Yakub Khan had made to me in New York. I had conveyed to him that third party involvement is irrelevant and redundant in the context of our bilateral relations as spelt out in the Simla Agreement. Improvement in our relations requires Pakistan taking credible measures to create confidence and demonstrate its seriousness about improving relations with India.

I also noticed that the Japanese Prime Minister, who is a very valued friend of India, was giving attention to the current tensions in our region. His well-meaning concern was welcomed. He appreciated India's position when he called for settling the differences peacefully through talks in accordance with the letter and spirit of the Simla Agreement.

Our official spokesman in his statement on 28 April 1990 and I shared with the media in London our surprise at the change in Pakistan's Foreign Minister's stand compared to the approach he had indicated to me during the New York meeting. I would rather not speculate on what his motivations could have been, but it would not be an unsafe guess to say that he had in his mind a hawkish home lobby. Several honourable members of Parliament had referred to Pakistani Foreign Minister's political leanings in his country. For us, this was not relevant; he was the Foreign Minister of the Government of Pakistan and I talked to him in that capacity.

The Government has time and again made it clear there can be no compromise on our stand that the State of Jammu and Kashmir is an integral part of India. Preceding Prime Ministers have categorically admitted this and our official spokesman clarified the position further. My reference to the fact that we would not tolerate infringement of our sovereignty and territorial integrity was obviously related to our principled stand on Jammu and Kashmir. This was clearly communicated in our reply at New York when the Pakistani delegation made a reference to Jammu and Kashmir in the Non-Aligned Meeting. We categorically stated that Jammu and Kashmir is an integral, inseparable part of India.

There was a general appreciation of India's stand by the world powers. These powers and the others have endorsed the Simla Agreement. The US Government has expressed itself against a plebiscite in Kashmir. It does not favour internationalization of the issue.

China expressed hope that India and Pakistan would remove differences and settle disputes through friendly consultations. All these countries expressed their support to resolving of differences between India and Pakistan through dialogue as indicated in the Simla Agreement.

While various Pakistani leaders said time and again that they

242

supported the Simla Agreement, in actuality, Pakistan was violating several of its (Simla Agreement) provisions. These included stipulations relating to prevention of the organized assistance or encouragement to any acts detrimental to maintenance of peaceful and harmonious relations. It also stipulated the prevention of hostile propaganda directed against each other. It called for respecting each other's territorial integrity and sovereignty and non-interference in each other's internal affairs. Pakistan's attempts to internationalize the Kashmir issue are also in violation of the provisions whereby the two countries must settle their differences by peaceful means or bilateral negotiations or any other peaceful means mutually agreed to between them.

It appeared to us that Pakistan hoped to make certain gains through overt and covert support to terrorism and by encouraging insurgency. Such ambitions were clearly based on wrong assumptions. Pakistan should be aware that we have the capacity to defend our sovereignty and integrity. We kept our communication channels open with Pakistan in the belief that it would realize that it is in their own larger interest that they abandon their misguided policies before they are overtaken by events.

In New York, I met a large number of Foreign Ministers from various parts of the world and virtually all of them appreciated India's position and expressed support for the Simla Agreement.

The BBC reports, reinforced what we had been saying. We had sufficient evidence regarding Pakistan's involvement and support to terrorism directed against India. Such evidence was provided to the Government of Pakistan. It was also confirmed by independent sources. Apart from the BBC other reliable commentators also highlighted Pakistan's support to terrorism. An article in *Washington Post* dated 23 April 1990, by Mr S Harrison said, 'Evidence obtained in Pakistan as well as through Indian and American intelligence sources indicate that sixty-three

Pakistan-operated camps have been functioning at various times during the past two years'. The *Time* magazine of 7 May 1990, called on Pakistan not to encourage secessionists.

There were also several reports indicating that some extremist groups in Kashmir had been in touch with the Afghan Mujahideens, obtaining weapons and training from them. There were also reports suggesting that some of these groups were participating in fighting against the Government of Afghanistan. We were carefully monitoring all this and planning appropriate counter-measures to safeguard our national interests.

We favoured the democratic process in Pakistan and were happy to see its consolidation. However, the policy of the Pakistan Government and various other elements in the Pakistani polity posed a danger to the political and democratic process in Pakistan itself. We believe in a meaningful cooperative relationship that will enhance the economic, cultural and political cooperation between countries.

Our pluralistic democracy discusses and occasionally differs on some issues, but when challenged, it has always risen to the occasion and responded unitedly. Pakistan is not only trying to cause disturbances in Punjab and Jammu and Kashmir, it primarily wants to disrupt our secular polity, the bedrock of our national unity. We are diverse in several ways, but the zeal of patriotism unites us. This is a moment when nothing should be said or done that might give an incorrect impression or may weaken the cherished institutions of our secularism and democracy.

IV

THE GULF CRISIS

32

The Gulf Crisis of 1990-91*

The Gulf War threw the country in the midst of a very deep crisis. The crisis did not pertain to India alone; the dangers were, in a way, affecting the entire world. It was very disappointing that this situation arose particularly when the Cold War had ended only about two or three months ago and when we were envisioning the future of the human race from a different perspective. India's stand on this issue was in conformity with its policy postulates framed by leading personalities like Mahatma Gandhi, the Father of our nation, and Jawaharlal Nehru. India is a country of great traditions that unify the nation in the hour of crisis.

During the Gulf War, every country was worried about the safety of its citizens and so our Embassy staff was supplemented to serve our people in distress. The Indian Foreign Service alone could not cope with it, as the repatriation of such a large number was a huge problem. It was difficult even to send a large number of planes because of the war environment prevailing in Iraq. The Iraqis were not in a position to open their airfield because of the UN restrictions. The air corridors were similarly closed and so the pilots were extra cautious. The UN restrictions allowed us

*Suo Moto statements on the Gulf War made in the Rajya Sabha on 23/8/1990.

247

to send our planes only up to Amman. We tried to persuade them to let some flights emanate from Baghdad and Basra but to no avail. The rehabilitation of such a large number of people posed a great challenge. It was not a question of a party or a particular government. The rehabilitation of a large number of people, who were used to a prosperous life and well paid jobs, was a difficult task. So, the rehabilitation of all sections of society needed both efforts and resources. We were trying to involve the public to mobilize funds on a volunteer basis. Fortunately, the people responded whole heartedly. Repatriation of such a large number is expensive, particularly because the planes go empty on outward journeys adding to the costs and burden on the exchequer. It is our great tradition that in an hour of crisis, we always do our best. We were hopeful that the situation would improve and the tension would end.

Prior to the crisis, a meeting of leading members of the Non-Aligned countries was fixed. It was to meet in Yugoslavia. After Iraq's attack on Kuwait added to all round anxieties, many members wanted to know as to how the NAM would respond. As I have said, we were deeply concerned and keen to lend our hand to end the critical situation. My colleagues in the Non-Aligned countries had similar concerns.

In order to be helpful and consistent with our traditions, we restrained our utterances. This was appreciated the world over. In this complex situation, we were keen to understand the situation before deciding what to do and how to achieve the desired goals. Some honourable friends wished to inquire about the assets left behind by our people. We worked out a scheme, whereby the customs would let people bring their jewellery and keep it in the safekeeping of bonded lockers at the airport and take it back when they return.

We had to close our Embassy in Kuwait because of obvious circumstances. The local authorities had notified all missions that electricity and water supplies would be disconnected and the diplomats would be denied diplomatic immunities after the notified day. Under the circumstances, we moved all our diplomats to Basra and augmented the Basra Consulate. We asked voluntary organizations to help our people and retained some of the local staff to render assistance to our citizens. The route via Shattul Arab in Iran was made available only to Iranian citizens and not to others. We requested the Iranian government to let our people also use the route but the response was unhelpful. As for the transfer of funds, the situation was such that no practical way out was available. A large number of our citizens in Baghdad also needed help.

We tried to organize airlifts from Baghdad but international insurance companies had stopped covering the risk. So sending flights of Air India into Iraq became difficult. We examined the possibility of using some other airports in addition to those already transporting people to Amman in Jordan but it did not seem feasible.

The safety and security of the large Indian community that was living and working not only in Kuwait and Iran but also in the adjoining areas of the United Arab Emirates and Saudi Arabia were our concern. We shared the agony of their families who were very worried. The agony of our people of Kerala where almost every home, every hearth was affected caused us deep sorrow. The wives and the mothers were worried about the bread-earners of their families who were far way. The possibility of a war breaking out caused anxiety to all of us. We arranged for transmission of information of the welfare of our people living in Kuwait to their near and dear ones in different parts of India. We also had to ensure inflow of petrol and petroleum products to keep the wheels of life moving.

About 6,000 people were in Amman while several thousands more were on their way while about ten thousand had already reached Baghdad from Kuwait. We were trying to engage ships to bring them home if the shipping companies would permit them to bypass the blockades. We fully adhered to the UN sanctions adopted by the Security Council (Resolution Number 661).

We were able to carry approximately 1,600 passengers everyday by air. The Air Force planes could bring in approximately 300 persons in one sortie. But clearance for using its airspace was not forthcoming from Iran.

It was the Indian Prime Minister who sent me to Kuwait and Iran to personally ensure the safety and security of our nationals.

When the Non-Aligned Ministers met, the Gulf crisis was foremost on our minds. The Non-Aligned bureau in New York had been meeting and keeping in touch with the UN. We all know that if there was a food shortage in Kuwait and Iraq, the first to suffer would be Asians—Indians, Pakistanis, Bangladeshis. That is why I tried to persuade the United States to let our food supplies through. We were trying to persuade the powers that were active in the blockade to understand our concerns.

The Government of India was not trying to mediate since mediation was feasible only when either of the two sides involved would seek it. We were for diffusion of the war like situation and were anxious to avert a crisis.

Iraq's invasion of Kuwait was certainly not justified. This is not the way diplomacy should be conducted, particularly in the post-Cold War era. The issue at the moment was not to apportion blames, the issue was how to difffuse the situation. Some countries chose in favour of military intervention, while some sent their armed forces.

The *Times* of London described the international armada already deployed in or en-route to Gulf as 'one of the largest assemblies of naval power in modern history'. It had already exceeded the NATO exercises in size and complexity. It was taking the world to the brink of war. Such a prospect was unfortunate. We do wish that the issue be resolved peacefully. Here I must say that we have a long history of close friendship with Kuwait. We expressed sympathy with the state of the people of

Kuwait who were victims of a wanton attack. We, therefore, supported the UN Resolutions that asked for immediate withdrawal of the Iraqi forces from Kuwait. Therefore, the Kuwait mission continued to enjoy all the privileges of a diplomatic mission in India. We continued to recognize the sovereignty of the Kuwaiti rulers over their territory.

33

The Safety and Repatriation of Indian Nationals During the Gulf War*

Indians were concerned about their fellow countrymen in Kuwait during the Gulf War. It was an issue which cut across parties. Our fellow citizens, our compatriots, who were approximately 2,00,000 in number, were living in Kuwait. They had made very remarkable contribution to the economy and life of that country. I think it was naturally the first duty of any government to look after and safeguard them and to see that the situation did not go to the extent that any one of them should get hurt. Our anxiety from the beginning had been roused and we had been trying to do whatever was humanly possible. But a few things may be kept in mind. The first thing was that there was a war-like situation. Therefore, all lines of communications had been snapped. There was no communication available; the airport had been closed; seaport had been closed; telephone lines had been disconnected and telegram facility had been withdrawn. Therefore, it was not possible to directly communicate with Kuwait.

All the same, we were constantly trying to get in touch with the situation of the country through indirect means. We had

*Statement delivered on the position of Indians in Kuwait on 9/8/1990.

tried all methods and there were standing instructions to all the Embassies of India throughout the world to try to get in touch with the host countries there and check up if any line of communication was available or not. We were constantly in touch with Iraq. Our entire Embassy in Baghdad was devoted to this task of keeping in continuous touch with the Iraqi Government. We were getting reports quite a few times a day. Therefore, the cell that had been set up was not only looking after the reports, complaints and enquiries that were coming in but also, at the same time, was keeping in constant touch. Fortunately, our Ambassador in Kuwait did a very ingenious thing, he was able to contact Nicosia on an amateur frequency and give us the information that all Indians in Kuwait were safe. This, by itself, was a matter of great satisfaction. We were trying to use that frequency again in order to keep in touch with them. The Government of Iraq had given us an assurance that orders had been issued to the military of Iraq to see that Indians were safeguarded by all means. They assured us that Indians were safe. This was the position as it stood then. I had given standing instructions that we should not take up the matter with the Iraqi Government. We were trying to persuade them and trying to see whether we could evacuate some people or not. There were several options available. One option was that we could possibly get the people out via Amman by road. But the only issue was whether or not their own security concerns would permit them to open the border of Amman. This was something on which our influence could not work. The people of Iraq, whether right or wrong, were trying to work out their own perception as to what would safeguard their interest. Therefore, this difficulty was there. We were exploring the possibility of evacuating Indians by sea and my instructions were that not only should we evacuate them by sea, if possible, but we need not bring all of them straight to India, because that would take more time. Even if we could take them to one of the adjoining Gulf countries, they would be safe but everything depended upon at what stage Iraq felt safe enough to reopen its airport or its seaport or re-establish communication systems. Minefields had also been laid because it was a war-like situation.

We spared no efforts, money, or means, which could possibly provide relief to our fellow citizens there. We were also trying various communication systems. Saudi Arabia had some sort of a wireless communication with Kuwait. The situation had taken a turn for the worse because the Americans had taken certain steps. As regards other aspects, the Security Council had passed a resolution for mandatory sanctions against Iraq. That concerned us also. Half of our oil was coming from Kuwait and Iraq put together and this had to be kept in mind when we took stock of the entire situation.

As far as bank transfers were concerned, the question of Indian banks not accepting Dinars did not arise, since the banks were not operational in Kuwait, any transfer that originated there was honoured in India.

Not only citizens of India but ethnic Indians who did not have Indian passports, were also our concern. We were doing everything humanly possible to see to it that their lives and interests were safeguarded. All of us had friends and relatives involved there. Though we had set up a cell, unfortunately, we were not in a position to give individual information. We had information that most Indians were safe, but it was not possible for me to get individual information. There were some cases which were of grave concern to us. For instance, one of the persons whom I knew very intimately was a lady who was in the advanced stages of pregnancy. All her relations and friends were worried about her. There were three sisters, young girls, of a family who were in the British Airways plane flying from London to Delhi which was detained in Kuwait. The family was naturally worried. I shared these anxieties. It was not a question of the government and the opposition. It was one of all of us being involved and all of us being concerned. I assured the nation that the government would not leave any stone unturned to come to their rescue.

34

Our Concerns During the Gulf War*

The deterioration of the situation in the Gulf was a cause of grave concern to all Indians cutting across party lines. I have already discussed how we sought the safety of Indians in Kuwait and the measures we took for their repatriation. We were also concerned that the situation be resolved in a peaceful manner. It was imperative in this situation that diplomatic initiative should be taken to resolve the crisis. The importance of the Non-Aligned Movement in taking an initiative in this regard was very evident. Mainly at our suggestion, Yugoslavia, the then Chairman of the Non-Aligned Movement, decided to establish a Group of three countries—Algeria, India and Yugoslavia—and convened a meeting of this group.

An important question discussed by me particularly during my visits to Moscow and Washington was that of the sale of oil supplies at a reasonable price. Over 40 per cent of our oil imports, including supplies from the former Soviet Union, originated in Iraq or Kuwait. The responses that I got during my discussions both in Moscow and Washington were generally encouraging. The American Foreign Secretary then Mr James

---

*Suo Moto statement delivered on 23/8/1990 on visit to Moscow, Washington, Amman, Baghdad and Kuwait in the context of the Gulf Crisis in Lok Sabha/Rajya Sabha.

Baker told me that the US supported the proposal for an increase of production by Gulf producers and others so that the overall shortfall, and its adverse effects on prices and availability, could be minimized. The Soviet Government immediately agreed to seek an alternative source for the supplies of oil which had hitherto originated in Iraq and said they would welcome a delegation from India to work out the details immediately. They also offered oil of Soviet origin, an offer which was examined to see if it could be availed.

There was also the overall question of the adverse effects on the economies of countries like India, due to the crisis in the Gulf, particularly of the application of the mandatory sanctions imposed by the Security Council. So far as the mandatory sanctions themselves were concerned, India naturally kept in step with the world community. However, in our inter-dependent world, severe or draconian measures applied in any part of the world cannot but have adverse effects on the rest of the world. The UN Charter had visualized this problem, though not to the extent that it was assuming and had provided for recourse to the Security Council with regard to the solution of any special problems that may arise. In my discussions in Moscow, the Soviet Government agreed that joint efforts were needed at the international level to ease the burden on countries like India which were severely affected by the Gulf Crisis. The subject was also discussed in Washington where I was told that the US also believed in international cooperation to ease the burden on countries like India which were most adversely affected. We had commenced consultations in New York with several countries, similarly affected, to explore the possibility of taking action through the UN.

There were other problems which were our major concerns such as the future of the Indian community, oil supplies and prices and the burden of sanctions. At the same time, we also had to think of possibilities that might de-escalate the crisis. Any measure for de-escalation would be in keeping with the general trend of recent years towards global detente and strengthening of peace.

We were also equally concerned about the destabilising effect of this crisis on our region. The Gulf region is a neighbour of South Asia. Escalation of tension or conflict there would have serious repercussions on us. We had already seen that Pakistan and Bangladesh had decided to send troops to the area of tension in the Gulf. This could very well be used as an excuse for further militarization of these countries, thus posing a threat to the security of the whole region. This made it incumbent upon all of us to look for openings for de-escalating and diffusing the tension.

I did not propose to assume a mediatory or good officer's role. I made this clear to all the leaders I met. Nevertheless, one of the objectives of the discussions was to find whether there was any chance of reversing the ongoing escalation of warfare. We tried to explore this tentatively at this stage and though my discussions during the tour did not reveal much of a meeting ground, it was imperative that our efforts to this end continued.

Clearly, humanitarian considerations were uppermost in our mind because of the large Indian community and people of other nationalities including Iraq and Kuwait who were adversely affected by the food shortages and other circumstances. As I had already stated, there was an agreement among all concerned that food supplies for humanitarian purposes could be sent. However, in the context of the interdiction policy, we were not sure whether it could really work. We were exploring the possibility of sending a shipload of food from India to alleviate the suffering of the people of all nationalities caught in the current crisis.

Immediately after the onset of the crisis, we expressed our regret that the differences between Iraq and Kuwait could not be settled peacefully and stated our well-known position against the use of force in any form in inter-State relations and called for the earliest possible withdrawal of Iraqi forces from Kuwait. At the same time, we expressed our disapproval of unilateral action outside the framework of United Nations by any country or group of countries to enforce the mandatory sanctions decided by the Security Council. We were also against the induction or presence of foreign military forces in this region.

It was our hope that the crisis in the Gulf would be reversed and the international community would see the wisdom of making a determined effort to diffuse the tension and restore peace and stability in the region. Both the Arab League and the Non-Aligned Movement had an important role to play in this regard.

Index